Game Development with Python

Game Development with Python

Kevin O'Flaherty
with Tom Stachowitz

LearnToProgram, Inc.
Vernon, Connecticut

LearnToProgram.tv, Incorporated
27 Hartford Turnpike Suite 206
Vernon, CT 06066
contact@learntoprogram.tv
(860) 840-7090

ISBN-13: 978-0-9904020-8-4
ISBN-10: 0990402088

Mark Lassoff, Publisher
Kevin O'Flaherty, Author
Tom Stachowitz, Technical Writer
Kevin Hernandez, VP/ Production
Alison Downs, Copy Editor
Alexandria O'Brien, Book Layout

Dedication:
To Barbie. After reading this book, you'll no longer need to turn to your friends Brian and Steve for help!

Courses Available from LearnToProgram, Inc.

3D Fundamentals with iOS
Advanced Javascript Development
AJAX Development
Android Development for Beginners
Become a Certified Web Developer (Level 1)
Become a Certified Web Developer (Level 2)
C++ for Beginners
C Programming for Beginners
Creating a PHP Login Script
Creating an MP3 Player with HTML5
CSS Development (with CSS3!)
Design for Coders
Game Development with Python
Game Development Fundamentals with Python
GitHub Fundamentals
HTML and CSS for Beginners (with HTML5)
HTML5 Mobile App Development with PhoneGap
Introduction to Web Development
iOS Development Code Camp

iOS Development for Beginners Featuring iOS6/7
Java Programming for Beginners
Javascript for Beginners
Joomla for Beginners
jQuery for Beginners
Mobile Game Development with iOS
Node.js for Beginners
Objective C for Beginners
Photoshop for Coders
PHP & MySQL for Beginners
Programming for Absolute Beginners
Project Management with Microsoft Project
Python for Beginners
Ruby on Rails for Beginners
SQL Database for Beginners
Swift Language Fundamentals
User Experience Design

Books from LearnToProgram, Inc.

Create Your Own MP3 Player with HTML5
CSS Development (with CSS3!)
HTML and CSS for Beginners
Javascript for Beginners
PHP and MySQL for Beginners
Programming for Absolute Beginners
Python for Beginners
SQL Database for Beginners
Swift Fundamentals: The Language of iOS Development

TABLE OF CONTENTS

About the Author:

Kevin O'Flaherty

Kevin has always been one to walk the unbeaten path. He discovered programming at age 13 and game development soon after. A couple years later he launched a website featuring tutorials and interactive resources for the Torque 2D engine. The resources can still be found at torquescripter.com.

Kevin received a Computer Science degree from Stony Brook University in 2013 and has since used his education and experience to jump head first into entrepreneurship, startups, and the web.

About the Technical Writer:

Tom Stachowitz

Tom Stachowitz was born in Florida but spent his childhood in northwestern Connecticut. He had always been interested in writing and technology but didn't begin programming until high school. Tom studied Journalism at the University of Indianapolis' overseas campus in Athens, Greece and, after living in England, Greece, New York, Arizona, Colorado, Washington DC, and Virginia and then serving in the Army, he returned to Connecticut to focus on writing and technology.

In his spare time Tom enjoys hiking, games, and spending time with his beautiful wife, Krista, and their two cats.

* Access the complete lab solutions for this book at:

https://learntoprogram.tv/book-lab-solutions

Thinking Like a Game Developer

Chapter Objectives:

- You will learn what a game loop is and why it is important.
- You will create your first game loop.
- You will capture player input and use it to modify the game state.
- You will learn how to manage lag and understand the importance of optimization.

1.1 First Game Loop

Welcome to Game Development with Python! In this book, we'll show you how to use the Pygame modules with Python to develop games and, more importantly, how to think like a game developer. We assume that you already have some knowledge of Python basics and that you understand how to get simple programs up and running. This way, we can jump right in and start developing games!

The goal of this book is to help you gain a solid understanding of theories and ideas that are integral to game development, and to be able to apply those to whichever programming language you are most comfortable with. We are using Pygame to achieve this goal, because Pygame is a fantastic lightweight and portable set of modules that is completely free. The games you develop with Pygame can be free, commercial, or anything in between. Once you've completed this book, you can continue with Pygame and Python or you can port your new knowledge and experience to any other platform.

> ### Game Loop
>
> The pattern of receiving player input, updating the game, and then rendering the game objects that the player is interacting with.

In this section we're going to look into the basic structure of a game, the **game loop**. Everything that your game does is going to be tied up in this game loop. The game loop is the pattern of receiving player input, updating the game, and then rendering the game objects that the player is interacting with. To demonstrate the game loop and to introduce Pygame, we will create a simple game loop that displays a game screen and then changes its background color.

We will be downloading Pygame from http://www.pygame.org. Throughout this book, we will be using Pygame version 1.9.1 with Python version 2.7.6 on the Microsoft Windows 7 operating system.

The Pygame website has a comprehensive set of documentation and tutorials that can be an exceptional resource while you're developing. There is also a large and active community of Pygame developers which serves as an invaluable resource to a new game developer.

Figure 1-1: The Pygame.org website.

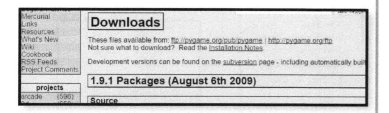

Figure 1-2: The Pygame download page. Ensure that you select the correct version and platform.

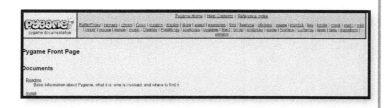

Figure 1-3: The Pygame documentation page.

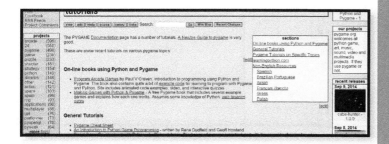

Figure 1-4: The Pygame Tutorial page.

1 Go to the Pygame website at:

http://www.pygame.org

2 On the left side of the page is the site menu. Select "Downloads."

3 On the Pygame download page, select the appropriate version of Pygame for your platform. If you want to follow the book exactly then install Python version 2.7.6 and Pygame version 1.9.1.

Pygame has comprehensive documentation and an extensive set of tutorials, shown in figures 1-3 and 1-4, that act as an invaluable resource for developers of any level.

4 Now we'll create a new Python file. Select "File" and then choose "New File."

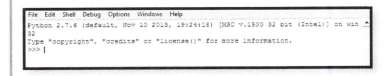

Figure 1-5: The IDLE Python shell.

5 Once you have a new, empty Python file, save it as "main.py."

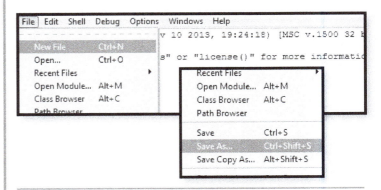

6 Now you're ready to start creating your first game loop!

Figure 1-6: Create a new Python file. Select "Save As."

We have chosen to save our files in a directory called "PyGame," but you can choose to save your Pygame files wherever is most convenient.

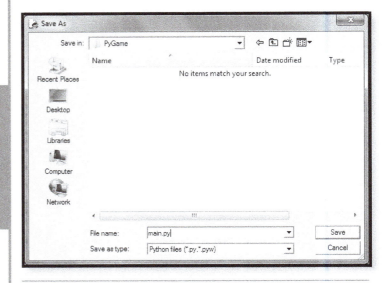

Figure 1-7: Save it as "main.py."

```
 ▹   import sys, pygame
 ▹   pygame.init()
 ▹   screen = pygame.display.set_mode(
     (800,600) )
```

Example 1-1: Create a simple gameplay window.

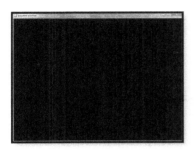

Figure 1-8: Our first game loop window is pretty boring.

```
 ▹   import sys, pygame
 ▹   pygame.init()
 ▹   screen = pygame.display.set_mode(
     (800,600) )
 ▹   screen.fill( (255,0,0) )
 ▹   pygame.display.flip()
```

Example 1-2: Using RGB values we can give it some color.

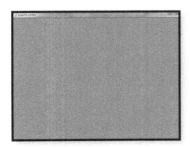

Figure 1-9: The gameplay window is now red.

7   Enter and run the code from code example 1-1. It will create a gameplay window named *screen* that is 800 pixels wide by 600 pixels tall. *screen* is a surface object in Pygame. We'll talk about surfaces later.

8   To give *screen* a color, enter and run the code from code example 1-2. The *screen.fill()* method takes an **RGB value** as an argument. Here, we're using the RGB value for red.

The **pygame.display.flip()** method is one of three methods available to refresh the Pygame display.

RGB Value

RGB stands for Red Green Blue, and is a standard way of defining color. Each value can be a number between 0 and 255, with 0 representing no color and 255 representing full color. For example, the RGB for black is 0,0,0 and white is 255,255,255.

Now let's change the red screen to yellow using our game loop.

9 First we're setting up variables to represent our RGB values, as in code example 1-3. Setting up variables will allow us to modify the values as the program runs.

10 Next, example 1-4 shows how we're creating our game loop. We want our game to continue until we explicitly close it, so we use an infinite WHILE loop.

11 Consider how to get from red to yellow. Red is RGB 255, 0, 0 and yellow is RGB 255, 255, 0. To get from red to yellow we have to increment our green value, shown in example 1-5.

12 Finally, set the color of *screen* to the values of our RGB variables and refresh the display, as in code example 1-6. With every loop iteration the display color will get closer and closer to yellow.

When you run the complete program, as shown in example 1-7, the screen will quickly change from red to yellow.

```
import sys, pygame
pygame.init()
screen = pygame.display.set_mode(
(800,600) )
red = 255
blue = 0
green = 0
```

Example 1-3: Setting up variables for the RGB values.

```
while True:
```

Example 1-4: Creating your game loop with WHILE.

```
green += 1
```

Example 1-5: Increment the value of the green variable.

```
screen.fill( (red,green,blue) )
pygame.display.flip()
```

Example 1-6: Set the screen color and update the display.

```
import sys, pygame
pygame.init()
screen = pygame.display.set_mode(
(800,600) )
red = 255
blue = 0
green = 0

while True:
    green += 1

    screen.fill( (red,green,blue) )
    pygame.display.flip()
```

Example 1-7: Our complete program.

Our application window changes color from red to yellow, but it does so very quickly. We are going to change that by defining the update speed of our game. We want our game to update at approximately 60 frames per second. Pygame has a few ways of specifying a frame rate, but for now we will use the **time.delay()** method. **time.delay()** causes execution to delay for a set number of milliseconds. We are also going to add some comments to make it more clear exactly what it is that we're doing.

By adding the code below we can add comments and implement **time.delay()**. The screenshots are only showing the code that is within the WHILE game loop.

```
#MAKE YOUR UPDATE HERE
green += 1

#RENDER CHANGES
screen.fill( (red, green, blue) )
pygame.display.flip()
```

Example 1-8: We've used some comments to organize the code.

```
#MAKE YOUR UPDATE HERE
green += 1

#RENDER CHANGES
screen.fill( (red, green, blue) )
pygame.display.flip()

pygame.time.delay(16) #60fps
```

Example 1-9: We've added a time delay to ensure that the game runs at 60 frames per second.

13 In example 1-8 we have added some comments to our code. As the program grows, this will make it easier to organize our code. We have separated the code that we are updating, in this case the value of *green*, from the code that renders our updated game.

14 In code example 1-9 we have added a **time.delay()**. This method takes a value in milliseconds as an argument, and we are passing 16 because that delay will approximate 60 fps.

Frames Per Second

Frames per second, or FPS, refers to the number of times a display updates every second.

If you've been keeping an eye on your shell as you've been working through this section, you probably noticed that an error keeps popping up. The error, shown in figure 1-10, is informing us that our color argument is invalid. Why would this have happened?

We set our value of green to increase with each iteration of the loop, so eventually it will reach a value higher than 255, the maximum for an RGB value. To fix this problem, we will have to set limits on the possible values of *red, green*, and *blue*.

15 Our error is caused by *green* being out of RGB range, so first check if *green* is greater than or equal to 255.

16 If *green* is greater than or equal to 255, set its value to 255. This will solve the immediate problem.

17 This problem may return if we change the other variable values, so replicate the logic to limit the values of *red* and *blue*.

18 Later we will want to have our color values go down as well as up, so use similar logic and ELIF statements to ensure that *red, green*, and *blue* stay above 0.

Your game loop should now look like example 1-10.

```
Traceback (most recent call last):
  File "C:\Users\Stack.Stack-PC\Desktop\PyGame\main.py", line 13, in <module>
    screen.fill( (red,green,blue) )
TypeError: invalid color argument
>>> |
```

Figure 1-10: Our initial implementation eventually results in an error.

```
while True:
    #MAKE YOUR UPDATE HERE
    green += 1
    if red >= 255:
        red = 255
    elif red <= 0:
        red = 0
    if green >= 255:
        green = 255
    elif green <= 0:
        green = 0
    if blue >= 255:
        blue = 255
    elif blue <= 0:
        blue = 0

    #RENDER CHANGES
    screen.fill( (red, green, blue) )
    pygame.display.flip()

    pygame.time.delay(16) #60fps
```

Example 1-10: The updated code resolves our error.

We now have a game loop, but it doesn't do very much. The application window's color changes to yellow, but once it turns yellow, it stays yellow. To make the game loop more interesting, we're going to have the color constantly shift and change.

To create this shifting color we're going to add two things to our game loop, more logic to the update section and a few more variables. We will create direction variables to control whether the RGB values increase or decrease, and then we will modify our loop logic to implement the new variables.

```
red = 255
redDirection = 1
blue = 0
blueDirection = 1
green = 0
greenDirection = 1
```

Example 1-11: Adding direction variables for each color.

```
if red >= 255:
        red = 255
        redDirection = -1
elif red <= 0:
        red = 0
        redDirection = 1
if green >= 255:
        green = 255
        greenDirection = -1
elif green <= 0:
        green = 0
        greenDirection = 1
if blue >= 255:
        blue = 255
        blueDirection = -1
elif blue <= 0:
        blue = 0
        blueDirection = 1
```

Example 1-12: Modifying the direction variables appropriately.

19 Add a direction variable for each color and assign them the value 1, as shown in code example 1-11. This direction variable will control if an RGB value is going to increase or decrease, with 1 causing an increase and -1 causing a decrease.

20 We want the RGB values to decrease after they have reached the maximum RGB value and increase when they are at the minimum RGB value, so we will set the values appropriately in our IF and ELIF statements. Code example 1-12 demonstrates implementing the conditionals in the game loop.

```
▸  red += 1 * redDirection
▸  green += 2 * greenDirection
▸  blue += 3 * blueDirection
```

Example 1-13: The modified RGB values.

21 Example 1-13 shows how we use the direction variables to either increment or decrement the color variables. We have also introduced a little variation in the values that we increment by in order to have some variety in the background.

22 Now, when our loop iterates each RGB variable will either increment by a set value or increment by that value multiplied by -1, effectively decrement the variable.

23 The IF ELIF logic ensures that no RGB variables will have a value outside of the allowable range. When those range limits are met, the logic will reverse the value of the direction variable.

24 In example 1-14 you can see the completed WHILE loop.

```
▸  #MAKE YOUR UPDATE HERE
▸  red += 1 * redDirection
▸  green += 2 * greenDirection
▸  blue += 3 * blueDirection
▸
▸  if red >= 255:
▸      red = 255
▸      redDirection = -1
▸  elif red <= 0:
▸      red = 0
▸      redDirection = 1
▸  if green >= 255:
▸      green = 255
▸      greenDirection = -1
▸  elif green <= 0:
▸      green = 0
▸      greenDirection = 1
▸  if blue >= 255:
▸      blue = 255
▸      blueDirection = -1
▸  elif blue <= 0:
▸      blue = 0
▸      blueDirection = 1
▸
▸  #RENDER CHANGES
▸  screen.fill( (red, green, blue) )
▸  pygame.display.flip()
▸  pygame.time.delay(16) #60fps
```

Example 1-14: The complete WHILE loop.

```
import sys, pygame
pygame.init()
screen = pygame.display.set_mode(
(800,600) )
red = 255
redDirection = 1
blue = 0
blueDirection = 1
green = 0
greenDirection = 1

while True:
    #MAKE YOUR UPDATE HERE
    red += 1 * redDirection
    green += 2 * greenDirection
    blue += 3 * blueDirection
    if red >= 255:
        red = 255
        redDirection = -1
    elif red <= 0:
        red = 0
        redDirection = 1
    if green >= 255:
        green = 255
        greenDirection = -1
    elif green <= 0:
        green = 0
        greenDirection = 1
    if blue >= 255:
        blue = 255
        blueDirection = -1
    elif blue <= 0:
        blue = 0
        blueDirection = 1

    #RENDER CHANGES
    screen.fill( (red, green, blue) )
    pygame.display.flip()

    pygame.time.delay(16) #60fps
```

Example 1-15: The final code for this section.

Example 1-15 shows the completed code for this section.

In this first section, we have introduced the idea of a game loop, showed how to create a simple game loop, and used simple logic within the game loop to update what is displayed.

In the next section, we will continue working with game loops and introduce player input.

WHAT HAVE YOU LEARNED?

Questions for Review:

1 What is a game loop?

a The pattern of receiving player input, updating the game, and then rendering the updates.

b Any large, repeated code block in a game.

c The feature in a game that lets a player start over after they lose.

d Any part of the game where a player is upside down.

2 In an RGB color value, what does the "G" stand for?

a Gradient.

b Grey.

c Green.

d Garish.

3 The following is a valid RGB value: (0,134,265)

a True.

b False.

4 What are Frames Per Second in video games?

a The amount of times the monitor is refreshed every second.

b The delay between game loops.

c The amount of time between the game updating and the screen rendering.

d The number of times the game is rendered each second.

1.2 A Simple Game Loop

In this section we will continue to examine game loops and introduce implementing player inputs. Our example will create a static window with a simple rectangle that the player can move using the arrow keys.

We will also introduce the Pygame event queue. The event queue is how Pygame handles all event messaging and it will allow you to interrupt your game loop in order to process player input, among other things.

```
import pygame, sys
pygame.init()
screen = pygame.display.set_mode(
(800,600) )
screen.fill( (200,200,255) )

pygame.display.flip()
```

Example 1-16: The application window that we create.

```
import pygame, sys
pygame.init()
screen = pygame.display.set_mode(
(800,600) )
screen.fill( (200,200,255) )

rectangle = pygame.Rect(0, 0, 60, 40)
pygame.draw.rect(screen, (255,255,255),
rectangle)

pygame.display.flip()
```

Example 1-17: The code to draw our rectangle. **pygame.draw. rect()** takes the name of the surface to draw on, the color of the drawn rectangle, and the name of the rectangle to draw.

1 Create a new python file and import pygame. Make an application window named *screen*.

2 Fill *screen* with the RGB value 200, 200, 255.

3 Remember to refresh the display using **pygame. display.flip()**! Example 1-16 shows how your code should look.

4 Create *rectangle* from the **pygame.Rect** class. **pygame. Rect** defines location with an X and Y coordinate and size with a width and height.

5 Use **pygame.draw. rect()** to draw *rectangle* to the screen. You can see the code in example 1-17.

We now have a simple, light blue screen with a white rectangle, as shown in figure 1-11. We will use this rectangle as the player-controlled element in our game loop.

6 First, position the rectangle near the center of the screen to make it clearly visible to players.

7 Create a WHILE game loop and put the rectangle rendering logic inside of it.

8 To ensure that our rectangle can move, within the game loop increment its X and Y position by accessing *rectangle.x* and *rectangle.y*.

Origin, or position 0,0 for the X and Y coordinates of a surface, is the surface's top left pixel. Increasing the X value of an object on that surface will position the object further right, and increasing the object's Y value will position it further down.

Figure 1-11: Our light blue screen with our rectangle.

```
import pygame, sys
pygame.init()
screen = pygame.display.set_mode(
(800,600) )
screen.fill( (200,200,255) )
rectangle = pygame.Rect(0, 0, 60, 40)

while True:
    #UPDATE GAME
    rectangle.x += 1
    rectangle.y += 1

    #RENDER CHANGES
    pygame.draw.rect(screen,
(255,255,255), rectangle)
    pygame.display.flip()
```

Example 1-18: Add a WHILE game loop containing the logic to move *rectangle*.

Figure 1-12: You'll notice that *rectangle* streaks across the screen.

You probably noticed that when the code from figure 1-12 ran, *rectangle* didn't move as you might have expected. Instead of traversing *screen* as a discreet object, it streaked along and left a trail. This happened because our game loop refreshes the display after *rectangle* has been rendered in a new location but does not re-execute *screen.fill()*.

It is the execution of *screen.fill()* that makes our application window, *screen*, the light blue color that we have chosen for our background. The code as it stands only fills the application window with color one time, and then the game loop renders *rectangle*. As the game loop renders *rectangle* multiple times it draws on top of the application window, which has already had *rectangle* drawn on it.

The result is that every render of *rectangle* in the game loop is displayed on top of one execution of *screen.fill()*, creating a streaking effect.

There is a simple solution to this problem, and that is to include *screen.fill()* in the game loop. Because we want *screen.fill()* to create our backround, it must be performed both before *rectangle* is rendered and before the display is refreshed.

```
    #RENDER CHANGES
    screen.fill( (200,200,255) )
    pygame.draw.rect(screen, (255,255,255),
    rectangle)
    pygame.display.flip()
```

9 Add *screen.fill()* to your game loop. *screen.fill()* is creating the background, so be sure that it executes before any other objects are rendered.

10 Example 1-19 and the two images following show what the render code in your game loop should look like. Now, *rectangle* will move properly.

Example 1-19: *rectangle* moves properly with this code.

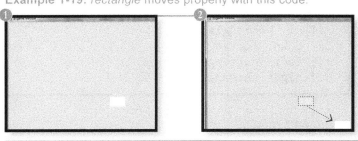

Now that we have *rectangle* moving properly, we can add player input. In order to process player input we will access the event queue. The event queue is a list of events and inputs from the player that Pygame stores until we decide to check them. We use the **pygame.event.get()** to check the event queue. Every input is stored in a list as an event object that we will create logic to test for.

Event Queue

The event queue is a list of player inputs stored as event objects that we can access with the **pygame. event.get()** function.

11 At the start of the game loop, get the events from the event queue so we can check them later, as shown in example 1-20.

```
while True:
    for event in pygame.event.get():
        if event.type == pygame.QUIT:
            sys.exit()
```

Example 1-20: Using **pygame.event.get()** to access the event queue.

12 The **pygame.key. get_pressed()** function returns an array of Boolean values representing the state of every key on the keyboard. We use it in example 1-21 to determine if an arrow key has been pressed.

```
#PROCESS PLAYER INPUT
up = pygame.key.get_pressed()[pygame.K_
UP]
down = pygame.key.get_pressed()
[pygame.K_DOWN]
left = pygame.key.get_pressed()
[pygame.K_LEFT]
right = pygame.key.get_pressed()
[pygame.K_RIGHT]
```

Example 1-21: Determining which key was pressed.

13 Modify the game logic so that the rectangle no longer moves automatically but moves in a particular direction when the appropriate arrow key is pressed, as shown in example 1-13.

Remember that an object's location is based on the origin, which is the top left pixel of *screen*.

```
#UPDATE GAME
if up: rectangle.y -= 1
if down: rectangle.y += 1
if left: rectangle.x -= 1
if right rectangle.x += 1
```

Figure 1-13: Moving *rectangle*.

If the code was entered correctly you should be able to control *rectangle* with your keyboard's arrow keys. Great job!

Your keystrokes are correctly moving *rectangle* because the *up, down, left*, and *right* variables are storing the state of the up, down, left, and right arrow keys. We can know the state of the arrow keys because **pygame.key.get_pressed()** returns an array of Boolean values that represent the state of every key on the keyboard. We then access the Boolean value stored in that array for the specific keys that interest us and set our variables to those values.

Once we have those key status values stored as variables, we use those variables as the basis for logical statements to determine how our game updates. In our simple example, the only thing that can change is the location of *rectangle*, so our logic simply changes the values of the X and Y coordinates of *rectangle*.

As you're moving *rectangle* around your game area, take a moment to test what happens when you attempt to move beyond the bounds of *screen*. You'll notice that *rectangle* continues moving until it's no longer visible. We don't want this to happen - instead, we want to ensure that *rectangle* remains visible at all times. To fix this problem, we will set limits to how far *rectangle* can move.

The technique that we will use is nearly identical to defining the limits of our RGB values in section 1.1, only instead of a color value limit, we'll be setting an X and Y coordinate limit.

```
#UPDATE GAME
if up: rectangle.y -= 1
if down: rectangle.y += 1
if left: rectangle.x -= 1
if right rectangle.x += 1

if rectangle.x <= 0:
rectangle.x = 0
if rectangle.y <= 0:
rectangle.y = 0
```

Example 1-22: This code ensures that *rectangle* does not go off the top or left side of *screen*.

14 We will add logic below our movement logic to check the location of *rectangle*. Keeping *rectangle* from going off the top or left of the screen is easy because we can just test against origin, shown in code example 1-22. Remember that the origin point for a rectangle and for a surface is the top left pixel.

15 To limit *rectangle* from going off the right or bottom side of *screen,* we need to stop its motion when it reaches the size of *screen* minus the size of *rectangle*. To do this, we calculate the width and height of *screen* with *screen.get_width()* and *screen.get_height()* and access the width and height of *rectangle* with *rectangle.width* and *rectangle.height*. Subtracting the width and height of *rectangle* from the size of *screen* gives us the variables *maxX* and *maxY* for use in our logic.

16 Once we have the maximum value for *rectangle*'s X and Y coordinates, implementing the logic to limit its movement is a simple matter of replicating the code for the minimum coordinates and modifying the conditional statement, as seen in code example 1-23.

```
#UPDATE GAME
maxX = screen.get_width() - rectangle.
width
maxY = screen.get_height() - rectangle.
height

if up: rectangle.y -= 1
if down: rectangle.y += 1
if left: rectangle.x -= 1
if right rectangle.x += 1

if rectangle.x <= 0:
    rectangle.x = 0
if rectangle.x >= maxX:
    rectangle.x = maxX

if rectangle.y <= 0:
    rectangle.y = 0
if rectangle.y >= maxY:
    rectangle.y = maxY
```

Example 1-23: The code to keep *rectangle* from moving beyond the viewable area.

Congratulations, you have created a simple game loop that takes player input, uses that player input to update the game state, and then renders those updates to the screen!

In the next section, we'll look at the importance of timing in your game and introduce a few small optimizations to get you thinking about concepts like performance and consistency.

Questions for Review:

1 What is the Event Queue?

a The event object between the Event P and the Event R.

b The list of events that need to occur in each game loop.

c The list of player inputs stored as an event object.

d The list of display outputs stored as an event object.

2 In Pygame, where is the origin position of a surface located?

a The exact center of the surface.

b The top left pixel.

c The bottom right pixel.

d The bottom left pixel.

3 What does **pygame.key. get_pressed()** return?

a A list of all the keys that are pressed.

b A boolean value if any key is pressed.

c A string of all the keys currently being pressed.

d An array with the boolean value of every key on the keyboard.

4 In order to ensure that the background renders appropriately, it must be rendered before any other element.

a True.

b False.

1.3 Understanding Frame Rates

In this section, we'll explore the impact that timing and frame rates have on your games and we'll introduce a technique to mitigate problems caused by lag.

Start by opening up the *rectangle* example that we have been working with. We're going to work with two techniques, **pygame.time.delay()** and **pygame.time.Clock()**.

1 First, we'll use **pygame. time.delay()**. This function adds a delay of a certain number of milliseconds to your game loop. Implement it as shown in example 1-24.

```
#RENDER CHANGES
screen.fill( (200,200,255) )
pygame.draw.rect(screen, (255,255,255),
rectangle)
pygame.display.flip()
pygame.time.delay(16)
```

Example 1-24: Using **pygame.time.delay()** to control timing in a game loop.

You'll notice that we passed the argument 16 to **pygame.time. delay()**. A 16 milisecond delay will approximate 60 FPS in our simple game. The problem with this is that it does not account for the processing time of the loop itself, so it will not be consistent.

```
import pygame, sys
pygame.init()
screen = pygame.display.set_mode(
(800,600) )
screen.fill( (200,200,255) )
rectangle = pygame.Rect(400,300,60,40)
clock = pygame.time.Clock()
```

Example 1-25: Initializing a clock outside of the game loop.

2 Next, we'll use **pygame. time.Clock()**. This initializes a clock object outside of our game loop, as in example 1-25, and allows us to define a FPS within our game loop, as in example 1-26.

```
#RENDER CHANGES
screen.fill( (200,200,255) )
pygame.draw.rect(screen, (255,255,255),
rectangle)
pygame.display.flip()
clock.tick(60)
```

Example 1-26: Setting the FPS with a clock in the game loop.

Using the **pygame.time.Clock()** class to create a clock object allows us to use the **tick()** method. The argument passed to **tick()** forces the game to run no faster than that number of FPS. With our simple game, this effectively locks the frame rate to 60 FPS. Experiment with different values for the **tick()** argument to see how various frame rates effect the feeling of your game.

You may find it useful to increase the speed with which *rectangle* moves. This is simply a matter of increasing the number of pixels that *rectangle.x* and *rectangle.y* is modified by in each frame.

When working with frame rates, keep in mind that most modern games have 60 FPS as a target and consider 30 FPS to be a minimum. Also, consider the type of games that you are interested in designing. Each frame will include not just how quickly elements are displayed, but how quickly inputs are processed. This will impact the feeling of the game and can be especially important in fast-paced action games. Finally, bear in mind that most monitors have refresh rates of 60HZ, which correlates to 60 FPS.

If you set the maximum FPS to 60, what happens if a game takes more than one sixtieth of a second to complete all of its processing? Our game is too simple to have this problem, but to demonstrate the problem, we will introduce random lag using Python's **random** library and the **pygame.time.delay()** function.

```
import pygame, sys, random
```

Example 1-27: Import random in your program.

3 First, import that **random** library along with **pygame** and **sys**.

```
#SIMULATE DELAY
randDelay = random.randrange(0,100)
pygame.time.delay(randDelay)
clock.tick(30)
```

Example 1-28: Include the delay simulation within your game loop.

4 Use **random.randrange()** to generate a random number and use that number in **pygame.time.delay()**. Ensure that the range includes values higher than the FPS.

Experiment with different random number ranges, including values that go well beyond the chosen frame rate. You'll notice that if the delay is not exceedingly large, you will still have a playable game. The larger the delay, though, the more difficult playing becomes. It's not long before something as simple as moving a rectangle around a screen is an exercise in frustration.

As you develop complex games you will have to manage potential slowdowns and delays. You won't have control over what other software a player may have running, and you cannot anticipate every situation where a player may encounter slowdown, but there are a few techniques that can mitigate some of the more obvious problems.

First, you can minimize lag by having your game loop do less work. This is not always an option, though. Another technique is to have your program calculate where game objects would be if there was no lag.

The biggest issue with lag is inconsistency. When the frames are being rendered at an inconsistent pace, the movement of game objects will also be inconsistent. To avoid this problem, we are going to calculate the location of objects based on where we would expect them to be after a certain amount of time if the game was not lagging.

To keep track of time, we will use **pygame.time.get_ticks()**.

---

5 Outside of your game loop, create a variable *totalTime* that is set to 0.

6 Before you process player input, create a variable for the difference in time between loop iterations, *timeChange*; update *totalTime*, and create a variable to calculate the number of frames that should have occured since the last loop, *velScale*.

```
    ...
    totalTime = 0

    while True:
        ...
        #PROCESS PLAYER INPUT
        timeChange = pygame.time.get_ticks()
    - totalTime
        totalTime = pygame.time.get_ticks()
        velScale = timeChange / 16
        ...
```

Example 1-29: Calculating how many frames would have rendered at our target frame rate.

```
for event in pygame.event.get():
    if event.type == pygame.QUIT:
        sys.exit()
#PROCESS PLAYER INPUT
timeChange = pygame.time.get_ticks() -
totalTime
totalTime = pygame.time.get_ticks()
velScale = timeChange / 16

up = pygame.key.get_pressed()[pygame.K_
UP]
down = pygame.key.get_pressed()
[pygame.K_DOWN]
left = pygame.key.get_pressed()
[pygame.K_LEFT]
right = pygame.key.get_pressed()
[pygame.K_RIGHT]
#UPDATE GAME
maxX = screen.get_width() - rectangle.
width
maxY = screen.get_height() - rectangle.
height
if up: rectangle.y -= 5 * velScale
if down: rectangle.y += 5 * velScale
if left: rectangle.x -= 5 * velScale
if right: rectangle.x += 5 * velScale
if rectangle.x <= 0: rectangle.x = 0
if rectangle.x >= maxX: rectangle.x =
maxX
if rectangle.y <= 0: rectangle.y = 0
if rectangle.y >= maxY: rectangle.y =
maxY
#RENDER CHANGES
screen.fill( (200,200,255) )
pygame.draw.rect(screen, (255,255,255),
rectangle)
pygame.display.flip()
#SIMULATE DELAY
randDelay = random.randrange(0,200)
pygame.time.delay(randDelay)
clock.tick(60)
```

Example 1-30: The current game loop.

(7) When you update the game, multiply the value that *rectangle* moves by *velScale*, which stores the number of frames that should have occurred since the last loop.

We know that our game is going to have delay and not run at 60 FPS, so we plan ahead. The **pygame.time.get_ticks()** function returns the number of milliseconds that have passed since **pygame.init()** was called. We use **pygame. time.get_ticks()** to store the time that a loop was iterated through as *totalTime*. In the next loop iteration, we calculate how long it has been since the previous iteration by finding the difference between the current time and *totalTime*, and storing that as *timeChange*. We then reset *totalTime*. Now we can determine how many iterations would have occurred at the target FPS by dividing *timeChange* by the number of milliseconds we expect a frame to take at our target FPS — 16, in this case. That value is stored as *velScale* and used later when positioning *rectangle*.

Code example 1-30 shows you what our game loop looks like.

It is important to think about performance and consistency when designing games. For example, even in our simple game loop we are doing much more work than we need to. We are redrawing the entire screen in every frame, even though the only thing that changes is *rectangle*. We will do a simple optimization to demonstrate one of the ways that you can improve the performance of your game loop. We will create a rectangle that is the same color as *screen* and the same size as *rectangle* and use that to redraw the background behind *rectangle* as it moves.

8 Outside of your game loop create a rectangle named *oldRect*, as shown in example 1-31. Its location doesn't matter, but it must be the same size as *rectangle*.

```
rectangle = pygame.Rect(400,300,60,40)
oldRect = pygame.Rect(400,300,60,40)
```

Example 1-31: Create *oldRect*, make sure it's the same size as *rectangle*.

9 Within your game loop and before you update the location of *rectangle* set *oldRect.x* and *oldRect.y* to the same value as *rectangle.x* and *rectangle.y*. Code example 1-32 shows this.

```
#UPDATE GAME
oldRect.x = rectangle.x
oldRect.y = rectangle.y
```

Example 1-32: Set *oldRect* to *rectangle*'s position.

10 When you render the changes draw *oldRect* to *screen* with the same RGB values as *screen*, and then draw *rectangle* to *screen*, as in example 1-33.

```
#RENDER CHANGES
pygame.draw.rect(screen, (200,200,255),
oldRect)
pygame.draw.rect(screen, (255,255,255),
rectangle)
pygame.display.flip()
```

Example 1-33: Draw *oldRect* first and give it the same color as *screen*.

11 Remove *screen.fill()* from your game loop, shown in code example 1-34, and execute it immediately after you instantiate *screen*.

```
screen = pygame.display.set_mode(
(800,600) )
screen.fill( (200,200,255) )
```

Example 1-34: Draw *screen* once, outside of the game loop.

```
import pygame, sys, random
pygame.init()
screen = pygame.display.set_mode( (800,600) )
screen.fill( (200,200,255) )
rectangle = pygame.Rect(400,300,60,40)
oldRect = pygame.Rect(400,300,60,40)
clock = pygame.time.Clock()
totalTime = pygame.time.get_ticks()
while True:
    for event in pygame.event.get():
        if event.type == pygame.QUIT:
            sys.exit()
    #PROCESS PLAYER INPUT
    timeChange = pygame.time.get_ticks() - totalTime
    totalTime = pygame.time.get_ticks()
    velScale = timeChange / 16
    up = pygame.key.get_pressed()[pygame.K_UP]
    down = pygame.key.get_pressed()[pygame.K_DOWN]
    left = pygame.key.get_pressed()[pygame.K_LEFT]
    right = pygame.key.get_pressed()[pygame.K_RIGHT]
    #UPDATE GAME
    oldRect.x = rectangle.x
    oldRect.y = rectangle.
    maxX = screen.get_width() - rectangle.width
    maxY = screen.get_height() - rectangle.height
    if up: rectangle.y -= 5 * velScale
    if down: rectangle.y += 5 * velScale
    if left: rectangle.x -= 5 * velScale
    if right: rectangle.x += 5 * velScale
    if rectangle.x <= 0: rectangle.x = 0
    if rectangle.x >= maxX: rectangle.x = maxX
    if rectangle.y <= 0: rectangle.y = 0
    if rectangle.y >= maxY: rectangle.y = maxY
    #RENDER CHANGES
    pygame.draw.rect(screen, (200,200,255), oldRect)
    pygame.draw.rect(screen, (255,255,255), rectangle)
    pygame.display.flip()
    #SIMULATE DELAY
    randDelay = random.randrange(0,300)
    pygame.time.delay(randDelay)
    clock.tick(60)
```

Example 1-35: The complete code example.

Code example 1-35 shows the completed code. If you have any problems use the code from example 1-35 as a reference to find any errors.

Take some time to experiment with the code to get a better understanding of the concepts introduced in this chapter. The game loop that you've created may be simple, but it demonstrates important ideas like player input, game updating, lag management, game optimization and clock management. All of these ideas will be expanded upon as you work through this book.

In the next chapter, we will look at using graphics that are more complicated than a simple rectangle. You will be introduced to sprites and image processing. You will also learn how to effectively manage your game assets.

Questions for Review:

1 How do you keep track of time in Pygame?

    a pygame.time.get_ticks()

    b pygame.time.get_time()

    c pygame.time.delay()

    d There is no way to keep track of time in Pygame.

2 Why is it important to consider optimizations in your game?

    a To ensure that your game runs as quickly as possible.

    b To maintain a playable experience for users.

    c To do as little work per game loop as possible.

    d All of the above.

3 What is the most straightforward way to avoid lag?

    a Lower the screen resolution.

    b Buy a faster computer.

    c Do less work per game loop.

    d Use cloud computing to make your game faster.

4 What is a good target frame rate for modern games?

    a 30.

    b 60.

    c 15.

    d 120.

CHAPTER 01 LAB EXERCISE

1) Create two paddles:

a) Draw two paddles to the screen and position them appropriately.

b) Process keyboard input. (The "w", "s", "up", and "down" key)

c) Move the paddles up and down. The paddle on the left moves with the "w" and "s" keys and the paddle on the right moves with the "up" and "down" keys.

d) Prevent the paddles from moving off screen.

2) Create a ball that:

a) Bounces off the top and bottom of the screen.

b) Bounces off each paddle.

c) Resets when passing the left or right of the screen.

Graphics to Sprites

Chapter Objectives:

- You will learn about surfaces in Pygame.
- You will understand how to manage and load graphical assets.
- You will learn how to process images on a per-pixel level.
- You will use custom sprite classes to organize and manage game assets.

2.1 Surfaces

In the first chapter, we introduced the concept of the game loop. The game loop is what allows your game to take user input, update the game state, and draw the game to the screen. In this chapter, we'll go into more detail about creating the graphics that your game draws. We will look at how Pygame handles graphics, how surfaces are used, and how to manage images and sprites.

We will begin with surfaces. You might not have realized it, but we have been using surfaces since the first section. The *screen* object that you have been creating to with **pygame.display.set_mode()** is a surface object. In Pygame, a **surface** is an object that is used to represent any image. Surfaces have a fixed resolution and pixel format.

We can create many more surfaces than just the initial application display. Create a new Python file and give it a name you can easily remember. We chose "surfaces.py."

Surface

A **surface** is an object that is used to represent any image. Surfaces have a fixed resolution and pixel format.

---

1 The first thing to do is to ensure that the pygame library is being imported properly and that pygame is being initialized.

```
import pygame
pygame.init()
```

Example 2-1: Import the pygame library and initialize it.

2 Create a display surface named *screen* with a resolution of 800 x 600 and set its color to white. Use **pygame.display.flip()** to update the window, as in code example 2-2.

```
screen = pygame.display.set_mode(
    (800,600) )
screen.fill( (255,255,255) )
pygame.display.flip()
```

Example 2-2: Create *screen*, set its color to white and display it.

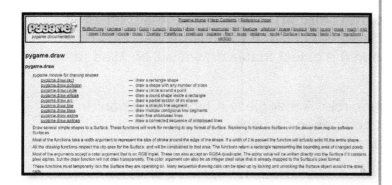

Figure 2-1: The documentation page for **pygame.draw** from http://www.pygame.org/docs/ref/draw.html

```
> screen = pygame.display.set_mode(
  (800,600) )
> screen.fill( (255,255,255) )
>
> pygame.draw.circle(screen, (0,0,255),
  (400,300), 100, 3)
>
> pygame.display.flip()
```

Example 2-3: The code to create a circle.

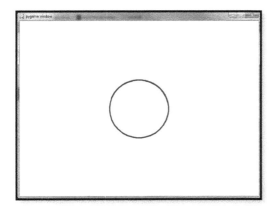

Figure 2-2: The result that you should see in your application window when you run the code.

3 You'll be looking at an empty Pygame window. To see the objects we can draw in that window, we'll refer to the Pygame documentation for **pygame.draw**.

4 In chapter one we worked with rectangles, but now we will begin by drawing a circle. Look at the documentation for **pygame.draw.circle()**.

5 The documentation informs us that we need to give our circle a surface to draw on, a color, a position, a radius, and a width. We know that *screen* is a surface, so we will use that as the first argument. Next, we will make our circle blue using RGB values. We will place the circle in the center of the screen, assign it a radius of 100, and assign it a width of 3. Example 2-3 shows the code to create this circle.

We are not creating a game loop to demonstrate drawing to surfaces, but feel free to create one as practice.

Note the width parameter of **pygame.draw.circle()**. We passed the argument "3" to define the width of the line that outlined our circle. If width is passed either the argument "0" or no argument at all, then the object that is drawn will be filled rather than outlined.

Next, we will draw a triangle within our circle. A triangle is a type of polygon. In Pygame, a polygon is a drawn object comprised of a series of points that are connected by lines. The final point connects to the first point, creating a closed shape.

```
screen = pygame.display.set_mode(
(800,600) )
screen.fill( (255,255,255) )
newSurface = pygame.Surface( (200,200) )

pygame.draw.circle(screen, (0,0,255),
(400,300), 100, 3)
pygame.draw.polygon(screen, (0,0,255),
[(400,300),(450,350),(475,325)], 3)

pygame.display.flip()
```

Example 2-4: Code to change a polygon into a triangle.

6 Look at the **pygame. draw.polygon()** reference. It defines a polygon as requiring a surface, a color, a list of points to define the polygon, and a width. Our polygon will be drawn on *screen*, it will be blue, and it will have a width of 3. We want the polygon to be a triangle, so the point list will include three sets of x,y coordinates. This list is defined within brackets, like so: [(x1,y1),(x2,y2),(x3,y3)]. Example 2-4 shows our code.

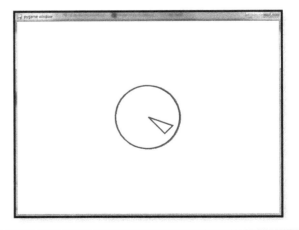

Figure 2-3: Our triangle polygon within our circle.

```
screen = pygame.display.set_mode(
(800,600) )
screen.fill( (255,255,255) )

offset = (100,100)

pygame.draw.circle(screen, (0,0,255),
(400,300), 100, 3)
pygame.draw.polygon(screen, (0,0,255),
[(400,300),(450,350),(475,325)], 3)

pygame.draw.circle(screen, (0,0,255),
(400 + offset[0],300 + offset[1]), 100,
3)
pygame.draw.polygon(screen, (0,0,255),
[(400 + offset[0],300 + offset[1]),(450
+ offset[0],350 + offset[1]),(475 +
offset[0],325 + offset[1])], 3)

pygame.display.flip()
```

Example 2-5: Adding the variable *offset* to display a second instance of the graphic.

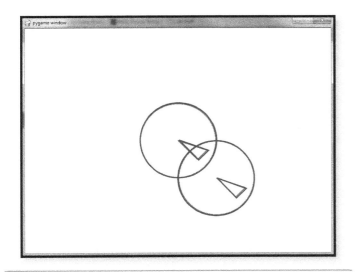

Figure 2-4: The code yields two instances of the graphic.

What do we do if we want to draw multiple instances of this graphic? When moving our rectangle from chapter one we modified the x and y coordinates of the object as needed. We can do something similar in the case of the simple circle and triangle graphic.

7 Create a variable called *offset* to hold a set of x,y coordinates. This will be where we want to display the second instance of the graphic. To keep our example simple, we will use the values (100,100).

8 Now, copy the code that we've created for our graphic and then modify the x and y position of each object by the appropriate offset value. Every x coordinate should have the value of offset[0] added to it, and every y coordinate should have the value of offset[1] added to it.

Example 2-5 and figure 2-4 show our code and the resulting display. Changing the offset values will change the location of the second graphic, but there's a lot of repetition in the code.

We're going to recreate our simple graphic using a new surface (which we will name *newSurface*) to introduce surfaces and demonstrate how useful they are. Remember that so far we have been drawing to the *screen* surface and so all of our coordinates have been relative to *screen*'s size. When we draw to a different surface, any coordinates will be relative to that surface instead of the application window.

If you look at the **pygame.Surface** class documentation on the Pygame website, you will find a long list of methods. We will not be covering all, or even most, of those methods in this book, but seeing them should give you a good idea of how useful surfaces are in Pygame.

Although we are not using a game loop in these examples, if you are, it's important to remember that you need to create and draw to *newSurface* outside of your game loop.

---

9 First, we will create *newSurface*. Surfaces are always rectangular, so when creating a surface object, you need a height and width parameter. Make *newSurface* a square with 200 pixel sides.

10 Recreate your simple graphic, only instead of passing *screen* as the surface argument, pass *newSurface*. When passing coordinate arguments, remember that these values are relative to *newSurface*, not *screen*. *newSurface* is only 200 by 200 pixels, so its center will be (100,100). Example 2-6 shows what your code should look like.

```
screen = pygame.display.set_mode(
  (800,600) )
screen.fill( (255,255,255) )
newSurface = pygame.Surface( (200,200) )

pygame.draw.circle(screen, (0,0,255),
  (100,100), 100, 3)
pygame.draw.polygon(screen, (0,0,255),
  [(100,100),(150,150),(175,125)], 3)

pygame.display.flip()
```

Example 2-6: We have created *newSurface* and we have drawn our graphic to it.

```
▷   screen.blit(newSurface, (0,0) )
▷
▷   pygame.display.flip()
```

Example 2-7: Using **blit()** to display *newSurface*.

Figure 2-5: **blit()** ignores the alpha channel and the graphic is displayed on a black background.

```
▷   newSurface = pygame.Surface( (200,200) )
▷   newSurface.set_colorkey( (0,0,0) )
```

Example 2-8: Setting black to transparent for *newSurface*.

Figure 2-6: The graphic displays without the black background.

If you run the code that you have, you will get an empty, white screen. Although our code creates *newSurface* and draws to it, we have not yet drawn *newSurface* to *screen*.

11 To display *newSurface,* we will use **pygame.Surface. blit()**. Using **blit()** will draw one surface onto another. As parameters, it takes the name of the source surface and the coordinate location of where to draw the source. When drawing, the origin of the source surface is drawn at the coordinates passed to **blit()**. Modify your code to use **blit()** before *screen* is displayed, as in example 2-7.

12 You'll notice that *newSurface* has a black background. **blit()** ignores the alpha values of pixels by default, but we can get around that by using **pygame.Surface. set_colorkey()**. **set_colorkey()** will set a color of a surface to be transparent whenever that surface is the source of a **blit()**. Use *newSurface. set_colorkey()* to make black transparent, as in example 2-8.

```
screen.blit(newSurface, (0,0) )
screen.blit(newSurface, (200,60) )
screen.blit(newSurface, (500,500) )
```

Example 2-9: Creating multiple copies of *newScreen* in various locations.

One useful feature of surfaces is their ability to be easily duplicated and displayed. In our previous example, duplicating our simple graphic required a substantial amount of repeated code. With surfaces, we can simply do another **blit()**.

13 Using *screen.blit()*, place multiple copies of *newScreen* in various locations around the application window. Figure 2-7 shows the result you may get.

BLIT is an acronym for BLock Image Transfer.

Figure 2-7: There are now three instances of the graphic placed in different locations around the application window.

Surfaces in Pygame give us very precise control over how, where, and when images and graphics are displayed.

In this section, we have worked with the primitive shapes available in Pygame. While many excellent games have been made using only primitive shapes, they are very limiting and represent only a fraction of what Pygame can do. In the next section, we'll begin using image files in our game to create an interesting and unique visual style.

Questions for Review:

1 What is a surface in Pygame?

a A platform that a player can jump or walk on.

b An object that is used to represent any image.

c An object that is automatically placed at the very bottom of the application window.

d The application window itself.

2 What does the width parameter of pygame.draw.circle() do?

a Defines the width of the entire circle.

b Defines the width of the surface that the circle is drawn on.

c Defines the width of the line that draws the circle.

d Nothing, there is no width parameter.

3 When drawing to a surface, what is the origin of the location coordinates for the source surface?

a The top left corner of the application window.

b The bottom left corner of the application window.

c The origin of the target surface.

d The center of the target surface.

4 What does pygame.Surface.blit() do?

a Draws one surface on to another surface.

b Replaces one surface with another surface.

c Removes the image data from a surface.

d Deletes a surface.

2.2 Working with Images

Now that we have a better understanding of how surfaces work in Pygame, we're going to begin using images with surfaces to create a more visually unique game. Designing graphics for games is a vast topic. Many talented artists spend years practicing and working to create the world you see when you load your favorite game. We are not going to cover graphic creation in this book, but in this section we will learn how to use graphical assets.

There are many exceptional resources available for aspiring game designers who need placeholder graphics in their games. We are going to use a sprite collection from http://www.lostgarden.com, although there are other sources to look at as you advance to other projects, including http://www.opengameart.org and http://www.yobi3d.com.

Most people make a very strong association between a game and its graphics, but keep in mind that graphics can be changed and improved throughout the development process. Placeholder graphics, even though they may not exactly match your vision, allow you to focus on core gameplay,ensuring that your game works as intended and is fun to play.

For this section, create a new folder in the location of your Pygames files called "images."

1 First we're going to obtain the art assets that we'll be using. Go to:

http://www.lostgarden.com

and click on the "Art" tab at the top of the screen.

Figure 2-8: http://www.lostgarden.com

Figure 2-9: The Lostgarden Art page.

Figure 2-10: We'll be using this graphics set.

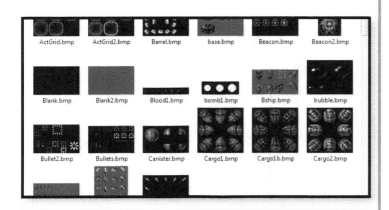

Figure 2-11: Downloaded, unzipped, and ready for use.

2 The art assets that we're going to use are towards the bottom of the page, but it's worthwhile to take a moment to look at what else is available. There are a variety of styles and some of the graphical assets that are available might inspire ideas for future projects.

3 The particular set that we are going to use is the Sinistar clone graphics set. It should be toward the bottom of the page. Download the graphics set and extract them in the "images" directory that you've created.

4 You'll see that there is an extensive set of graphics available, but for the moment, we're only interested in the files "Nebula1.bmp" and "Hunter1. bmp." Take some time to look through the rest of the graphics in the set, though, to get a sense of the game we'll be creating.

5 The particular files that we're interested in are Nebula1.bmp and Hunter1.bmp, shown in figure 2-15.

Figure 2-12: Nebula1.bmp and Hunter1.bmp

6 Create a Pygame application with *screen* having a resolution of 800 by 600. The first thing we will do is load the images into Pygame with **pygame.image.load()**, as shown in code example 2-10.

```
import pygame
pygame.init()

screen = pygame.display.set_mode(
(800,600) )
background = pygame.image.load("images/
Nebula1.bmp")
playerAsset = pygame.image.load("images/
Hunter1.bmp")
```

Example 2-10: Loading the images we intend to use.

7 When we load an image, we are creating a surface from the source image data. Use *screen.blit()* to display *background*. The results are shown in code example 2-11.

```
screen.blit(background, (0,0))
```

Example 2-11: Displaying *background*.

You've probably noticed that *background* isn't a background, so much as it's a lonely little image hiding in the corner of our window. This is because the surface that we created when we loaded Nebula1.bmp is the same size as the source image file. The graphical assets that we're using were not designed for modern, high resolution displays. To fix that problem, we're going to use Pygame's transform functions. A transform operation is how we modify surfaces in Pygame.

Figure 2-13: The *background* positioned at the 0,0 coordinates.

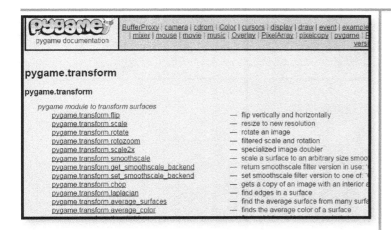

Figure 2-14: Pygame's transform documentation.

```
▷  background_stretched = pygame.transform.
    scale(background, (800,600))
▷
▷  screen.blit(background_stretched, (0,0))
```

Example 2-12: Using pygame.transform.stretch() returns a new surface that we can then display on screen.

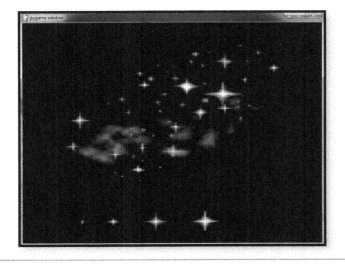

Figure 2-15: The background is stretched to fit the window.

(8) First, open up the Pygame transform documentation at http://www.pygame.org/docs/transform.html. It's good to have a reference available when you're working.

(9) We are going to use pygame.transform.scale() on background. Pygame transform operations all take a surface as an argument and return a surface. To implement pygame.transform.scale(), enter the code shown in example 2-12.

You'll notice that we didn't actually modify background. Instead, we created background_stretched and assigned it the result of the transform, then we modified screen.blit() to display the new surface. The other argument that we passed to pygame.transform.scale() was the size that we wanted to scale background to.

Note that we did not match the aspect ratio of Nebula1.bmp with background_stretched, so the image is visibly stretched. In this case that isn't a problem, however, as a general rule you want to scale proportionally.

10 Now that we have a background, we will add the player ship. Use *screen.blit()* to display *playerAsset* on the screen, as shown in figure 2-20. Remember that *playerAsset* has to be displayed after (or on top of) the background or it will not be visible.

11 The image displayed where we intended it to, but the original file is a sheet that contains the ship facing in multiple directions. This was often done because rotating an image is more processor-intensive than simply displaying a new image. To only use part of the image, we will use a feature of **blit()** that allows us to clip out a certain segment of the source surface, shown in figure 2-21.

The values passed to **blit()** after the source surface and location is the area we want to display, defined by a rectangle. The values, (25,1,23,23), clip out an area that starts at coordinate 25, 1 on the source surface and has a width and height of 23. We can determine those values by examining the source image in any image editing software.

```
screen.blit(background_stretched, (0,0))
screen.blit(playerAsset, (0,0))
```

Example 2-13: Using *screen.blit()* to display *playerAsset* over the background.

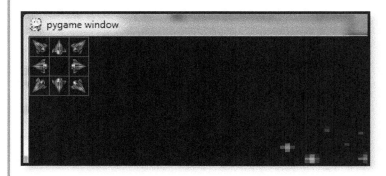

Figure 2-16: *playerAsset* is displayed overtop the *background*.

```
screen.blit(playerAsset, (0,0),
    (25,1,23,23))
```

Example 2-14: Using *screen.blit()* with a clipping rectangle.

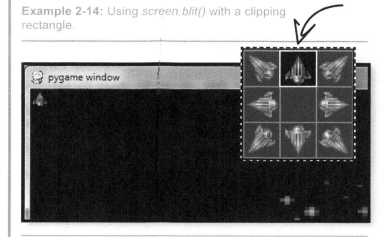

Figure 2-17: *playerAsset* is clipped so only one ship is showing.

```
def imageLoader(image, scale, clip):
```

Example 2-15: Define a function that takes an image source, a scale value, and a clip rectangle.

```
asset = pygame.image.load(image)
assetClipped = pygame.Surface(
    (clip[2],clip[3]) )
```

Example 2-16: Create a locally scoped variable *asset* to store the image source, and then create a surface for the clipped image.

```
assetClipped.blit(asset, (0,0), clip)
return pygame.transform.
scale(assetClipped, (clip[2] * scale,
clip[3] * scale) )
```

Example 2-17: Clip out only the desired part of *asset* and then return it, scaled appropriately.

```
playerSurface = imageLoader("images/
Hunter1.bmp", 2, (25,1,23,23))
screen.blit(playerSurface, (0,0) )
```

Example 2-18: Use *screen.blit()* to display the result of the *imageLoader()* function.

Figure 2-18: The ship image is displayed as desired.

We have code that correctly displays the part of our source image that we want, but it's specific to one file and would be unwieldy to replicate. We'll place that code into a function that returns a surface that displays only the useful part of an image.

12 Create a function called *imageLoader* that takes the parameters *image*, *scale*, and *clip*. *image* will be the location of the source, *scale* will be the value we want to scale the surface by, and *clip* will be the area of the source image we want.

13 In the function, set a variable *asset* to the image source, and then create a surface that is the size of our return surface. This will be the width and height of our *clip* parameter.

14 **blit()** the desired part of *asset* to the new surface, and then use **pygame.transform. scale()** to return a surface that is scaled according to the *scale* parameter.

15 Call the function and display the resulting surface.

As you saw in figure 2-18, we used the scale parameter of our function to double the size of the ship graphic. Our complete program is displayed below, in example 2-19. We define a function to display an image, then we create the application window with the *screen* surface. Next, we load the background and scale it to the appropriate size. Then we **blit()** the scaled background onto *screen*. Next, we use our function to load only the section of the Hunter1.bmp image that we intend to use for our player's ship, and finally we **blit()** that image onto *screen*.

Before we close out this section, we'll go over another **pygame.transform** function, **pygame.transform.rotate()**. As with the other transform operations, **pygame. transform.rotate()** takes an input surface and returns a new surface. It's important to note that rotating a rectangular surface any angle other than 180 degrees, or 90 degrees in the case of a square, will return a new surface that has larger dimensions than the original surface.

```
import pygame
pygame.init()

def imageLoader(image, scale, clip):
    #Load an image, clip the desired section, scale it appropriately
    asset = pygame.image.load(image)
    assetClipped = pygame.Surface( (clip[2],clip[3]) )
    assetClipped.blit(asset, (0,0), clip)
    return pygame.transform.scale(assetClipped, (clip[2] * scale, clip[3] *
scale) )

screen = pygame.display.set_mode( (800,600) )

background = pygame.image.load("images/Nebula1.bmp")
background_stretched = pygame.transform.scale(background, (800,600) )
screen.blit(background_stretched, (0,0) )

playerSurface = imageLoader("images/Hunter1.bmp", 2, (25,1,23,23) )
screen.blit(playerSurface, (0,0) )

pygame.display.flip()
```

Example 2-19: Our completed code thus far.

```
playerSurface = imageLoader("images/
Hunter1.bmp", 2, (25,1,23,23) )

playerRotated = pygame.transform.
rotate(playerSurface, 30)

screen.blit(playerRotated, (0,0) )
```

Example 2-20: The use of **pygame.transform.rotate()**

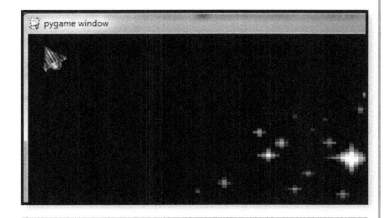

Figure 2-19: The ship appears rotated.

16 Use **pygame.transform. rotate()** to create a new surface called *playerRotated*. The function takes a surface and an angle. In this example, we'll rotate the image by 30 degrees.

17 Modify your code to display *playerRotated* instead of *playerSurface*, using **blit()**. Your results should match figure 2-19.

In this section we've used our knowledge of surfaces to begin using images to create a graphically interesting game. We also learned how to use transform operations in order to modify surfaces in our program.

In the next section, we'll look at some image processing transform operations and we'll learn how to directly modify pixels on a surface.

We will be returning to the code from this section in section 2.4, so be sure to save it.

WHAT HAVE YOU LEARNED?

Questions for Review:

1 What should you keep in mind when creating your game?

  a The graphics must be final before you begin to do any further development.

  b No one actually cares about graphics so you can just use squares and circles.

  c Placeholder graphics that may not exactly match your vision are very useful when developing core gameplay concepts.

  d You can not change your graphics once you have started implementing them.

2 What does pygame. transform.scale() do?

  a Takes a surface argument and returns a new surface that is a scaled version of the source surface.

  b Takes a surface argument and scales it.

  c Creates a new surface that is covered in scales.

  d Transforms the default scale value of Pygame.

3 You can use pygame.surface.blit() to crop out a part of the source surface.

  a True.

  b False.

4 Transform operations in Pygame never return a surface.

  a True.

  b False.

2.3 Image Processing

In this section, we are going to look at how we can process images in Pygame. We are able to access and modify the individual pixels of a surface, opening up a world of post-processing effects that can help create a unique visual style.

In order to learn more about image processing, we will need a test image. In computer science, the "Lenna" image, a crop from the centerfold of Lena Söderberg in a 1972 issue of Playboy, has long been used as the "hello world" of image editing. "Lenna" was originally used in 1973 when engineers needed a good image to showcase a photo scanner. The image was chosen because it was glossy, had good dynamic output range, featured a human face, and — most importantly — was available in the lab. Since then "Lenna" has become a standard test image for image processing.

Figure 2-20: "Lenna" on Wikipedia.

① The safest way to download "Lenna" is to go to Wikipedia, at http://www.wikipedia.org/wiki/Lenna. There you'll find some history about the image, as well as notes on the controversy around "Lenna."

② Click on the thumbnail image on the right side of the screen, and then click on the actual image to download "Lenna."

③ Save "Lenna" into your "images" directory.

Figure 2-21: The original 512x512px test version.

Now that you have a good test image to use, we can begin to process it. We haven't had to use a game loop while testing surfaces and learning how to access images, however, we will need to create a game loop in order to process images. From now on, we will be using a game loop for every example we create.

Before we begin processing "Lenna," we will create a template game loop that can be used as the basis for future examples, exercises, or programs.

4 First, import and initialize pygame.

5 Next, create an application window named *screen* that's 800 by 600 pixels.

6 Create a clock variable to keep track of timing.

7 Create a game loop outline and parse the event queue.

8 Ensure that your game loop handles the quit event appropriately.

9 Within your game loop, ensure that you refresh the display.

10 Finally, ensure that you set the clock ticks appropriately.

```python
# Game Loop Template
import pygame

pygame.init()

#Create the application window
screen = pygame.display.set_mode(
(800,600) )

#Create the game clock
clock = pygame.time.Clock()

#The game loop
while True:
    for event in pygame.event.get():
        if event.type == pygame.QUIT:
            pygame.quit()

    #Handle player inputs

    #Perform game logic

    #Update game state

    #Display game updates
    pygame.display.flip()
    clock.tick(60)
```

Example 2-21: Template Game Loop.

```
lenna = pygame.image.load("images/Lenna.
png")
#Create the application window
screen = pygame.display.set_mode(
(lenna.get_width(), lenna.get_height())
)
```

Example 2-22: Set the size of *screen* to match the size of the image we will be working with.

```
#Display game updates
screen.blit(lenna, (0,0) )
pygame.display.flip()
```

Example 2-23: Use *screen.blit()* to display our image within the game loop.

Having a template to start from is useful and will save us time, but the template is not set in stone. For example, we will immediately modify the size of *screen* in order to fit the application window to the size of the image that we will be working with.

11 The first thing we will do is load the image and assign it to a variable *lenna*.

12 Next we will set the size of *screen* to match the size of *lenna* using *lenna.get_width()* and *lenna.get_height()*. This is shown in code example 2-22.

13 Use *screen.blit()* within the game loop to display *lenna*, as shown in code example 2-23.

Figure 2-22: *lenna* is displayed.

```
  ▸  screen.blit(pygame.transform.
     laplacian(lenna), (0,0) )
```

Example 2-24: Appling the laplacian transform to the image.

14 The Pygame documentation's "transform" section shows us the image processing tools that are built into Pygame. We will use **pygame. transform.laplacian()** to do edge detection on *lenna*. Because every transform operation returns a surface, we can use this operation as an argument for *screen.blit()*. Modify *screen.blit()* from step 13 as shown in code 2-24.

Figure 2-23: Laplacian edge detection has a neat effect.

15 Another transform operation that we can test on *lenna* is **pygame.transform.average_ color()**. This operation will return a color that is the average of all of the colors from every pixel on a surface. We do not want to **blit()** this value because it is not a surface. Instead, we will use *screen.fill()*. Comment out the code from step 14 and add the *screen.fill()* shown in example 2-25. You can see that we used **pygame.transform. average_color()** as an argument because it returns a color object that *screen.fill()* can accept.

```
  ▸  screen.fill(pygame.transform.average_
     color(lenna) )
```

Example 2-25: Applying the average color transform.

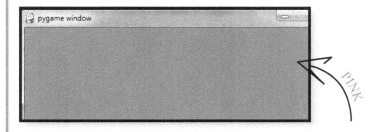

Figure 2-24: The average color of the surface.

The operations we have been using in this section so far have used the values of individual pixels on a surface to achieve an effect. We do not need to rely on only these functions to modify pixels, though. We can access the pixel array of a surface and then modify it ourselves.

To demonstrate this, we will create our own post-processing effect. First, we will verify that we can access the pixel data, and then we will apply our effect and display it to the screen.

```
lennaPixelArray = pygame.
PixelArray(lenna)
```

Example 2-26: Create an array of all of the pixels of the surface *lenna*.

```
for x in range(0, lenna.get_width()):
    for y in range(0,
            lenna.get_ height()
            ):
        print lennaPixelArray[x,y]
```

Example 2-27: Loop through the *lennaPixelArray* array and print the pixel data.

```
Python 2.7.6 Shell*
File  Edit  Shell  Debug  Options  Windows  Help
3411022
3608396
3805774
2819911
3212872
3738957
3739214
3279183
3543381
4134745
```

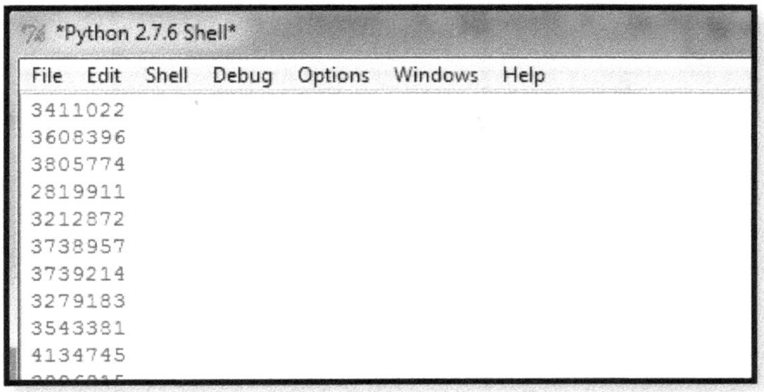

Figure 2-25: A close-up of the beginning of the loop data.

16 To access the individual pixel data we will first create an array to hold all of the relevant information. This array will be called *lennaPixelArray* and we will create it using **pygame.PixelArray()**, as shown in code example 2-26.

17 Once we have the array, we will loop through it to access each pixel's data. We are interested in the x and y coordinates, so use the size of the image and build a nested loop that will iterate through the entire array.

18 In order to verify that we can access the color data of each pixel, print the data from each pixel to the console. You will get a large list of color hexadecimal values, shown in figure 2-25.

Now that we can access the image's pixel color data, we are going to use those values in our program.

We know that *screen.fill()* takes a color value, so we'll begin with that. In the following example we are going to fill the screen with the color of the pixel at coordinate x, y in *lennaPixelArray*. In this example we are rendering to the screen multiple times every frame, which is not something we would want to do in our game, but we are doing it here for illustrative purposes.

19   Within the loop you created in step 17, add a variable, *pixel*, and assign to it the value of *lennaPixelArray[x,y]*.

```
pixel = lennaPixelArray[x,y]
screen.fill(pixel)
pygame.display.flip()
```

Example 2-28: This will fill the screen with the color of each pixel in *lenna*.

20   Use *screen.fill()* to set the color of the application window to *pixel* and then **flip()** the display. Example 2-28 shows the code. Remember, because you are rendering to the screen in this loop, you do not need to use **flip()** again later in the game loop.

You will see the application window flashing through different colors. As written, this code is not displaying all of the colors of each pixel to the user in sequence, but it is using the color values from *lenna* to fill the screen. Next, we will use these techniques to apply a custom per-pixel filter to *lenna*.

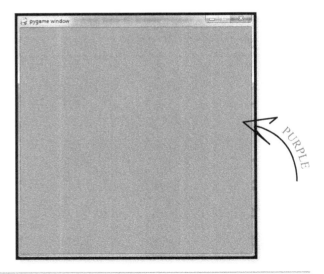

Figure 2-26: The screen will fill with each pixel color. This screenshot shows the screen filled with the color purple as one of the pixels from the image is purple.

This example will iterate through every pixel in the "Lenna" image and then use a conditional to determine if any given pixel should be modified. Here we are using web color hex triplets to represent colors. A hex triplet is a three-byte hexadecimal number where each hexadecimal byte is in the range of 00 to FF, which correlates to the range 0 to 255 in decimal notation. The bytes represent the RGB values we have used so far.

```
if pixel > 0x444444:
    lennaPixelArray[x,y] = 0xFFFFFF
```

Example 2-29: Test if a pixel is greater than 0x444444.

```
#Update game state
newLenna = lennaPixelArray.make_
surface()
screen.blit(newLenna, (0,0) )
```

Example 2-30: Display the modified pixels.

21 Remove the *screen.fill()* and **flip()** from the loop and replace them with a conditional that tests if *pixel* has a value greater than 0x444444. That notation refers to the hex triplet for dark gray.

22 If it does, set the pixel value to 0xFFFFFF. The hex triplet FFFFFF is RGB 255, 255, 255, which is white.

23 In order to display the modified pixels, we need to convert the pixel array to a surface. In the "Update game state" section of your loop, create a surface *newLenna* and assign it the result of *lennaPixelArray.make_surface()*.

24 Finally, **blit()** *newLenna* to the screen and **flip()** the display.

Figure 2-27: The Lenna image is displayed with the modified pixel coloration.

Figure 2-27 shows what Lenna should look like now.

```
# Game Loop Template
import pygame
pygame.init()
lenna = pygame.image.load("images/Lenna.png")
lennaPixelArray = pygame.PixelArray(lenna)
#Create the application window
screen = pygame.display.set_mode( (lenna.get_width(), lenna.get_height()) )
#Create the game clock
clock = pygame.time.Clock()
#The game loop
while True:
    for event in pygame.event.get():
     if event.type == pygame.QUIT:
            pygame.quit()
    #Perform game logic
    for x in range(0, lenna.get_width()):
     for y in range(0, lenna.get_height()):
            pixel = lennaPixelArray[x,y]
            if pixel >'0x444444:
                lennaPixelArray[x,y] = 0xFFFFFF
    #Update game state
    newLenna = lennaPixelArray.make_surface()
    screen.blit(newLenna, (0,0) )
    #Display game updates
    pygame.display.flip()
    clock.tick(60)
```

Example 2-31: The completed code example for this section.

After working through the examples, your code should look like the code in example 2-31. It will load an image onto a surface, create an array containing the color data for every pixel of the surface, loop through that array and make modifications according to the game logic, convert the array back to a surface, and finally display that surface on the screen.

In the next section we will return to our space scene and add more game assets. We will learn how to manage those assets and how to better organize our code.

Questions for Review:

1 What does pygame.
transform.laplacian() return?

    a The average color of a surface.

    b Basic edge detection of a surface.

    c Nothing.

    d The most dominant
color of a surface.

2 How can we access the color data
from individual pixels of a surface?

    a With surface.transform.get_pixels().

    b By creating a new surface from
each pixel and then using pygame.
transform.average_color().

    c By accessing the pixel array
with pygame.PixelArray().

    d We cannot access data from
individual pixels of a surface.

3 What is a hex triplet?

    a Macbeth's downfall.

    b A method of copying three
surface objects at once.

    c A three byte hexadecimal number
which correlates to an RGB value.

    d None of the above.

4 A surface can be created
from a pixel array.

    a True.

    b False.

2.4 Managing Game Assets

In this section, we are going to be returning to the space game code from section 2.2. Load the file that you saved at the end of that section. We are going to assume that the file is named main.py.

In section 2.2, we were only working with two assets, but as our game grows we will have to deal with more assets and more instances of game objects. In this section, we will learn how to organize our code to better manage our game assets.

It is very useful to get into the habit of organizing your code in a consistent and logical manner. Well organized code will save you time while developing, make it easier to find and fix errors, and will make your code more readable. It also promotes code portability and reduces repetition.

If you are using IDLE, note that you need to ensure that every file you are importing is saved and up to date before running your program from main.py. When you run a program, IDLE will prompt you to save it before it runs, however, this pop up only concerns the file being run, not imported files.

In this section, we will begin working with **sprites**. Sprites are two-dimensional images that are intended to be a part of a larger scene and can be manipulated without modifying the overall scene. The term "sprite" comes from early hardware implementations of graphics in computing. Images that could be manipulated by the player would not be a part of the bitmap data that comprised the background and would instead be drawn on top of it, "floating" over the environment as a ghost or spirit might. Even though computing advanced, the terminology stuck.

Sprites

Sprites are two-dimensional images that are a part of a larger scene and that can be manipulated without modifying the overall scene.

Many modern implementations of sprites package them with relevant functionality that handles display, movement, collision, and other gameplay elements. The Sprite class in Pygame is a lightweight class that provides a useful scaffolding for game objects, but still allows developers to maintain control.

The first thing that we are going to do is put our code from section 2.2 into our template from section 2.3 to ensure that we are using a game loop. Code example 2-32 shows you how the resulting code should look. Note that we removed the rotation of *playerSurface*.

```python
# Game Loop Template
import pygame
pygame.init()

def imageLoader(image, scale, clip):
    asset = pygame.image.load(image)
    assetClipped = pygame.Surface( (clip[2], clip[3]) )
    assetClipped.blit(asset, (0,0), clip)
    return pygame.transform.scale(assetClipped, (clip[2] * scale, clip[3] * scale) )

background = pygame.image.load("images/Nebula1.bmp")
background_stretched = pygame.transform.scale(background, (800,600) )
playerSurface = imageLoader("images/Hunter1.bmp", 2, (25,1,23,23) )

#Create the application window
screen = pygame.display.set_mode( (800,600) )

#Create the game clock
clock = pygame.time.Clock()

#The game loop
while True:
    for event in pygame.event.get():
     if event.type == pygame.QUIT:
            pygame.quit()

    #Handle player events
    #Perform game logic
    #Update game state

    #Display game updates
    screen.blit(background_stretched, (0,0) )
    screen.blit(playerSurface, (0,0) )
    pygame.display.flip()
    clock.tick(60)
```

Example 2-32: Our display code integrated into our game loop template.

1 First, create a new .py file and save it as imageLoader.py.

2 Copy the *imageLoader()* code into this new file and then comment *imageLoader()* out of main.py.

3 Ensure that imageLoader.py imports Pygame. imageLoader.py should match example 2-33.

4 To use this function in your main.py file, you need to import imageLoader.py, shown in example 2-34.

By using the wildcard character, as shown in example 2-34, you will have access to every function in the referenced file as if it were a part of main.py. You could instead specify the function to import. *****

5 Save imageLoader.py and run main.py to verify that it still functions, and then remove the commented out code.

```
import pygame

def imageLoader(image, scale, clip):
    asset = pygame.image.load(image)
    assetClipped = pygame.Surface(
(clip[2],clip[3]) )
    assetClipped.blit(asset, (0,0), clip)
    return pygame.transform.
scale(assetClipped, clip[2]*scale,
clip[3]*scale) )
```

Example 2-33: The imageLoader.py file.

```
import pygame

from imageLoader import *

pygame.init()

#def imageLoader(image, scale, clip):
    #asset = pygame.image.load(image)
    #assetClipped = pygame.Surface(
(clip[2], clip[3]) )
    #assetClipped.blit(asset, (0,0),
clip)
    #return pygame.
transform.        scale(assetClipped,
(clip[2]*scale,clip[3]*scale) )
```

Example 2-34: The modified main.py

```
▸   import pygame
▸
▸   class Background(pygame.sprite.Sprite):
```

Example 2-35: The gameObjects.py file and the Background class.

```
▸   def __init__(self, image, width,
    height):
```

Example 2-36: Our Background class will require an image, a width, and a height.

```
▸   self.originalAsset = pygame.image.
    load(image)
▸   self.image = pygame.transform.
    scale(self.originalAsset, (width,height)
    )
▸   self.rect = self.image.get_rect()
```

Example 2-37: The logic in our Background class is nearly identical to what we had in main.py.

6 We do not want to have game objects scattered around our code, so create a new file called gameObjects.py and ensure that it imports Pygame.

7 First, we will recreate our background. Create a Background class that extends Sprite, as shown in code example 2-35.

8 We need to create our class constructor. Consider what we need our Background class to do: display an image scaled to an appropriate size. Our constructor, then, will take an image file, a width, and a height, as shown in example 2-36.

9 Recreate our background logic from main.py in gameObjects.py, as in example 2-37. Note that we have added a rectangle as an attribute, *self. rect,* using *self.image.get_rect()*. Pygame's built-in Sprite class has methods that use an object's *rect* attribute so it is important to ensure that it exists.

10 In main.py, create an instance of Background using the same image file, Nebula1.bmp, from section 2.2. Code example 2-38 shows this. Note that we have used *screen.get_width()* and *screen.get_height()* for the width and height. It is good to avoid hard-coding values whenever possible to make code more portable.

11 In your display code where you **blit()** *background_stretched* to *screen*, modify the code so that you are displaying *background.image* instead. Also, for the x and y coordinates of the **blit()**, use the values stored in *background.rect*, as in example 2-39.

12 When you run main.py, your screen should be identical to what it was when you completed section 2.2, shown in figure 2-28.

Congratulations, you've created a Sprite object! We'll continue extending the Sprite class to create the player, enemies, and asteroids.

```
background = Background("images/Nebula1.
bmp", screen.get_width(), screen.get_
height() )
```

Example 2-38: Instantiate a Background object called background with our Nebula1.bmp graphic.

```
screen.blit(background.image,
(background.rect.x,background.rect.y) )
```

Example 2-39: Display the *image* attribute of *background* to *screen*.

Figure 2-28: If everything went well, your application window should look like this screenshot.

```
class Player(pygame.sprite.Sprite):
    def __init__(self, image, scale,
clip):
```

Example 2-40: Create a Player class in gameObjects.py

```
self.image = imageLoader(image, scale,
clip)
self.rect = self.image.get_rect()
self.rect.x = 400
self.rect.y = 300
```

Example 2-41: The content of the Player constructor

```
player = Player("images/Hunter1.bmp", 2,
(25,1,23,23) )
```

Example 2-42: Instantiate player in main.py

```
screen.blit(player.image, (player.
rect.x, player.rect.y) )
```

Example 2-43: Display player.image on screen.

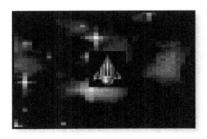

Figure 2-29: The ship image has a black square around it.

13 Before we create our Player class we need to import imageLoader.py into gameObjects.py so that we can access *imageLoader()*.

14 In gameObjects.py, create a Player class that extends Sprite. Build its constructor according to example 2-40.

15 In the body of your Player constructor, recreate the code used to load an image, as shown in example 2-41. Note that we have created *self.rect* for our Player class and set specific values for *self.rect.x* and *self.rect.y*. This is only for the purposes of testing.

16 In main.py, create an instance of Player called *player*, shown in example 2-42, and **blit()** it to *screen* as you did with *background* in step 11, shown in example 2-43. Note how your ship has a black square around it that obscures *background*. This is not new, but we haven't noticed it because of the location where we have been drawing our player ship.

```
def __init__(self, image, scale, clip,
ckey):
    self.image = imageLoader(image,
scale, clip)
    self.image.set_colorkey(ckey)
    self.rect = self.image.get_rect()
    self.rect.x = 400
    self.rect.y = 300
```

Example 2-44: Modify the constructor of your Player class to take a color parameter, *ckey*.

```
player = Player("images/Hunter1.bmp", 2,
(25,1,23,23), (0,0,0) )
```

Example 2-45: Use the appropriate color as an argument when instantiating *player*.

That may be frustrating, but if you recall section 2.1, then you know what's happening and how to fix it. We just have to use *player.image.set_colorkey()* to make black transparent. We can do this for *player* specifically, but it would be better to make the change in the Player class. Also, we may use a different image for a player object that may require a different transparency, so we should pass a color key as an argument to the class constructor.

17 Modify your Player class to add a color key parameter, as shown in example 2-44.

18 We know that the color that needs to be transparent is black, so modify the instantiation of *player* to pass the appropriate RGB value. Your player ship should now display properly, as shown in figure 2-30.

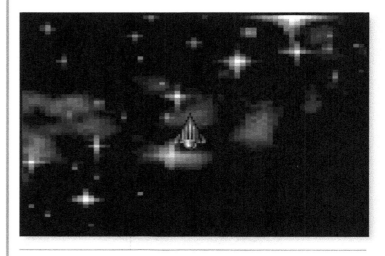

Figure 2-30: The ship image displays properly because the black is transparent.

72   *Game Development with Python*

```
class Enemy(pygame.sprite.Sprite):
    def __init__(self, image, scale,
clip, ckey):
        self.image = imageLoader(image,
scale, clip)
        self.image.set_colorkey(ckey)
        self.rect = self.image.get_rect()
        self.rect.x = 200
        self.rect.y = 500

class Asteroid(pygame.sprite.Sprite):
    def __init__(self, image, scale,
clip, ckey):
        self.image = imageLoader(image,
scale, clip)
        self.image.set_colorkey(ckey)
        self.rect = self.image.get_rect()
        self.rect.x = 100
        self.rect.y = 400
```

Example 2-46: Class definitions for Enemy and Asteroid in gameObjects.py

```
enemy = Enemy("images/SpacStor.bmp", 1,
(101,13,91,59), (69,78,91) )
asteroid = Asteroid("images/Rock2a.bmp",
1, (6,3,80,67), (69,78,91) )
```

Example 2-47: Instantiating an Enemy and Asteroid object in main.py.

```
screen.blit(enemy.image, (enemy.rect.x,
enemy.rect.y) )
screen.blit(asteroid.image, (asteroid.
rect.x, asteroid.rect.y) )
```

Example 2-48: Displaying *enemy* and *asteroid* in main.py.

Now that we understand how to extend the Sprite class, it will be simple to add enemies and asteroids to our game. Both enemies and asteroids will be added as extensions of the Sprite class, but will use different image assets.

We have already chosen the assets to use and the clipping areas for each sprite.

19 Create the Enemy and Asteroid classes, both of which extend Sprite. The bodies of these classes will be identical to Player, with the only differences being in their *self.rect.x* and *self.rect.y* values. Example 2-46 demonstrates what your code should look like.

20 In main.py, instantiate an enemy and an asteroid, as in example 2-47. You'll notice that the transparent color is gray instead of black. The value of this color is dependent on the source material. In the display section of your code, **blit()** the objects to *screen*, as shown in example 2-48.

Once you've instantiated the objects and rendered them, your screen should look like figure 2-31. This works well, but we are repeating rendering code to display our objects. There is functionality built into Pygame to render collections of sprites, but we will not be using that. Instead, we will create a rendering loop ourselves.

21 After you instantiate the game objects in main.py, append them to an array called *gameObjects*, as in example 2-49.

22 In the display section of your game loop, create a **for in** loop to iterate through *gameObjects*, rendering each object to *screen* in turn. This loop is shown in example 2-50.

This is where using *self.rect.x* and *self.rect.y* in the class definitions pays off. Setting and accessing the location of any game object is simple and consistent.

```
gameObjects = []
gameObjects.append(background)
gameObjects.append(player)
gameObjects.append(enemy)
gameObjects.append(asteroid)
```

Example 2-49: After instantiating your game objects in main.py, create an array *gameObjects* and append to it each game object we are going to display.

```
#Display game updates
for gameObject in gameObjects:
    screen.blit(gameObject.image,
(gameObject.rect.x, gameObject.rect.y) )
```

Example 2-50: Loop through *gameObjects* and display the objects on *screen*.

```
import pygame
from imageLoader import *

class Background(pygame.sprite.Sprite):
    def __init__(self, image, width, height):
      self.originalAsset = pygame.image.load(image)
      self.image = pygame.transform.scale(self.originalAsset,
                                          (width,height)
                                          )
      self.rect = self.image.get_rect()

class Player(pygame.sprite.Sprite):
    def __init__(self, image, scale, clip, ckey):
      self.image = imageLoader(image, scale, clip)
      self.image.set_colorkey(ckey)
      self.rect = self.image.get_rect()
      self.rect.x = 400
      self.rect.y = 300

class Enemy(pygame.sprite.Sprite):
    def __init__(self, image, scale, clip, ckey):
      self.image = imageLoader(image, scale, clip)
      self.image.set_colorkey(ckey)
      self.rect = self.image.get_rect()
      self.rect.x = 200
      self.rect.y = 500

class Asteroid(pygame.sprite.Sprite):
    def __init__(self, image, scale, clip, ckey):
      self.image = imageLoader(image, scale, clip)
      self.image.set_colorkey(ckey)
      self.rect = self.image.get_rect()
      self.rect.x = 100
      self.rect.y = 400
```

Example 2-51: The complete gameObjects.py file.

```
# Game Loop Template
import pygame, sys
from gameObjects import *

pygame.init()

#Create the application window
screen = pygame.display.set_mode( (800,600) )

#Create the game objects
background = Background("images/Nebula1.bmp", screen.get_width(),
                        screen.get_height()
                        )
player = Player("images/Hunter1.bmp", 2, (25,1,23,23), (0,0,0) )
enemy = Enemy("images/SpacStor.bmp", 1, (101,13,91,59), (69,78,91) )
asteroid = Asteroid("images/Rock2a.bmp", 1, (6,3,80,67), (69,78,91) )

#Create the objects collection
gameObjects = []
gameObjects.append(background)
gameObjects.append(player)
gameObjects.append(enemy)
gameObjects.append(asteroid)

#Create the game clock
clock = pygame.time.Clock()

#The game loop
while True:
    for event in pygame.event.get():
     if event.type == pygame.QUIT:
            pygame.quit()

    #Display game updates
    for gameObject in gameObjects:
     screen.blit(
                gameObject.image, (gameObject.rect.x, gameObject.rect.y)
                )
    pygame.display.flip()
    clock.tick(60)
```

Example 2-52: The complete main.py file.

```
import pygame

def imageLoader(image, scale, clip):
    asset = pygame.image.load(image)
    assetClipped = pygame.Surface( (clip[2],clip[3]) )
    assetClipped.blit(asset, (0,0), clip)
    return pygame.transform.scale(assetClipped,
                             (clip[2]*scale, clip[3]*scale)
                             )
```

Example 2-53: The complete imageLoader.py file.

Now you have all of the objects that you need to make a game! You have learned how to create and display a player, an enemy, and an asteroid. You have also learned how to manage game assets and how to manipulate images on a per-pixel level.

It's important to be able to manage and display graphical assets, but a collection of pretty graphics that don't actually do anything will not make for an interesting game. In order to have a game that users will actually want to play, you need to implement some logic to make your objects mobile and interactive. That is our next objective.

In the next chapter, you will learn about game physics and collision detection. We will go over simple physics, implement player inputs for our game objects, use thrust to create momentum and, finally, we will implement collision detection.

Questions for Review:

1 What are sprites?

a Any small image used in game development.

b Textures applied to surfaces.

c Large images often used for backgrounds.

d 2D images that are a part of a larger scene and that can be manipulated without modifying the overall scene.

2 When extending the Sprite class, why is it useful to include *self.rect* attribute?

a There is no reason to include *self.rect*.

b To be able to easily manipulate the object's height and width.

c Because Pygame's Sprite class has methods that use the *self.rect* attribute.

d To be able to delete a Sprite quickly.

3 The Sprite class should only be used for player controlled objects.

a True.

b False.

4 The Sprite class has built-in methods that can be useful when designing in Pygame.

a True.

b False.

CHAPTER 02 LAB EXERCISE

How you manage your surfaces will make a big difference when it comes to the performance of your game and how cluttered your code is. In this lab exercise, you'll be merging two images to create the player ship below. It is also a good idea to pack complex objects like the player ship into contained game objects using Sprites. That will be a part of this exercise.

1 Load the ship and weapon images:

　　a) ShipGun2.bmp

　　b) Hunter1.bmp

2 Draw the player ship:

　　a) Create a new surface to be used as the final surface for the game object.

　　b) Blit the weapons and ship to the surface. Make sure the ship is on top.

3 Make a player ship sprite:

　　a) Make a new sprite to hold this game object.

　　b) When the sprite is created, draw the ship and set it as the sprite's image.

Physics
and Collision
Detection

Chapter Objectives:

- You will learn about surfaces in Pygame.
- You will understand how to manage and load graphical assets.
- You will learn how to process images on a per-pixel level.
- You will use custom sprite classes to organize and manage game assets.

3.1 Simple Game Physics

Two of the earliest games were Spacewar and Pong. It might be hard to imagine if you're accustomed to the high-fidelity, eye-popping games of today, but both of those early games were simulations — Pong was a simulation of tennis, and Spacewar was a simulation of space combat. Game developers have long been working to simulate reality in their projects, and a key component of that simulation is physics. Physics is the thread that can be traced from the planned 2016 release of Star Citizen all the way back to 1962's Spacewar.

In this chapter we are going to implement physics for our space game, although our physics will be more like Spacewar than Star Citizen.

We are now accustomed to using the game loop and we have a working game loop template that loads a number of objects and displays them in a scene. We will continue to use our game loop to do the heavy lifting for us. We only need to concern ourselves with the small changes that happen each time our game loop iterates. Those small changes that we are concerned with are the updates that will be happening to our objects and the game state.

This update gives us a good place to start understanding physics. The first thing that we will do is consider what needs to be updated in each object during each iteration of the game loop.

1 First, open main.py and gameObjects.py. We are going to start by creating an update method in our game objects.

2 In the Player class, define a new method named *update()*, as shown in code example 3-1. This is where we will put everything that we want to change about Player when the game updates.

```
def update(self):
    #Process player input

    #Collision detection

    #Update physics
```

Example 3-1: In the Player class of gameObjects.py, create an update method. We have added comments to create a shell for our method.

```
def update(self):
    #Process player input

    #Collision detection

    #Update physics
    self.rect.x += 1
    self.rect.y += 1
```

Example 3-2: Using *self.rect.x* and *self.rect.y* to move a Player object in gameObjects.py.

```
#Update game state
player.update()
```

Example 3-3: In the update section of the game loop in main. py, call *player.update()*.

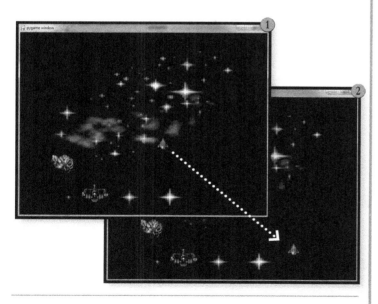

Figure 3-1: The ship object will slowly move down and right until it is off of the screen.

Consider how we will be simulating physics in our 2D game. We will need our objects to change their x and y coordinates in every game loop iteration. Our first goal should simply be to make that happen. We will do this within the "Update physics" section of *Player. update()*.

3 The simplest way to make our object move is to increment its x and y coordinates. We display our objects based on *self.rect.x* and *self.rect.y*, so if we modify those values we will modify the object's position. See code example 3-2.

4 In main.py we need to run the *Player.update()* method for our instance, *player*. Enter the code to do that in the "Update game state" section of our game loop, as shown in code example 3-3.

When you run the game you should see the player ship moving slowly down and to the right, eventually vanishing from view.

At the moment our physics system is very simple and only acts on one object, but the concept works. We are using an object's x and y coordinates to change its position over time by performing an update in every iteration of the game loop. We can increase the complexity of our simulation by making modifications to the update method that we have created.

The first modification that we will make is to update our physics using an attribute, rather than a set value.

5 In the Player class constructor, add two attributes, *self.velocityX* and *self.velocityY*. Set the initial value of *self. velocityX* to 3 and the initial value of *self.velocityY* to 1.

```
self.velocityX = 3
self.velocityY = 1
```

Example 3-4: In the Player class constructor, create and set two new attributes.

6 In *Player.update()*, increase the *self.rect.x* value by *self. velocityX* and increase the *self. rect.y* value by *self.velocityY*.

```
#Update physics
self.rect.x += self.velocityX
self.rect.y += self.velocityY
```

Example 3-5: In the Player class update method, modify your code to use the new attributes.

If you were to run this code now, you still see your player ship moving off of the screen, but the difference is that its movement is now being controlled by attributes.

Movement based on a static variable is a start, but we want to do something more interesting. Next, we will implement acceleration. Acceleration is the increase in an object's rate of speed.

7 First zero, out the velocity values in the constructor.

8 Create two new attributes, *self.accelerationX* and *self.accelerationY*.

We will add our acceleration value to the object's velocity in every game loop iteration. If we use a large value for acceleration, then the velocity value will become very large, very quickly. The Player object will simply hurtle off of the screen as soon as we load the program. To avoid this, we will set acceleration to a very low value.

9 Set *self.accelerationX* and *self.accelerationY* to 0.1, as shown in code example 3-6.

10 In your *Player.update()* method, set the velocity attributes to increase by the value of the acceleration attributes. In this way, every game loop will accelerate your object. This is shown in code example 3-7.

```
self.velocityX = 0
self.velocityY = 0
self.accelerationX = 0.1
self.accelerationY = 0.1
```

Example 3-6: The velocity and acceleration attributes in the Player class constructor.

```
#Update physics
self.velocityX += accelerationX
self.velocityY += accelerationY
self.rect.x += self.velocityX
self.rect.y += self.velocityY
```

Example 3-7: The physics updates in the *Player.update()* method after implementing acceleration.

When you run the program now you will see the player ship begin moving slowly down and to the right. Over time its velocity will increase until it is no longer visible on the screen. Congratulations, you've just implemented acceleration!

Now let's add an update method for all of the classes in gameObjects.py.

The update methods you will add to the Enemy and Asteroid classes will be identical and will be functionally similar to what currently exists in the Player class.

```
self.velocityX = 0
self.velocityY = 0
self.accelerationX = 0
self.accelerationY = 0
```

Example 3-8: Create attributes for acceleration and velocity in the Asteroid and Enemy classes and set them to 0.

11 Create attributes in Enemy and Asteroid to control velocity and acceleration, as shown in code example 3-8.

12 Add *update()* to Enemy and Asteroid as the code in example 3-9 shows.

```
def update(self):
    self.velocityX += self.accelerationX
    self.velocityY += self.accelerationY
    self.rect.x += self.velocityX
    self.rect.y += self.velocityY
```

Example 3-9: Include an update method in the Asteroid and Enemy classes that can move the objects.

13 For the Background class we will add an update method, but it will be empty and return nothing. We are doing this to maintain consistency with our objects and because we may, in future, want our Background objects to update. Code example 3-10 shows you what the *Background.update()* should look like.

```
def update(self):
    return
```

Example 3-10: Include an empty update method in the Background class.

Now every object in our game has an update method, however, the only update method that is called is for the Player class. The purpose of our objects' update methods is to contain all of the code that we intend to update in each iteration of the game loop, so we need to ensure that every game object has their update method called within the game loop.

Implementing this is easy because we have ensured that our classes have followed a standard naming convention and that they all include the required update method.

```
#Update game state
for gameObject in gameObjects:
    gameObject.update()
```

Example 3-11: Loop through all of the update methods of every game

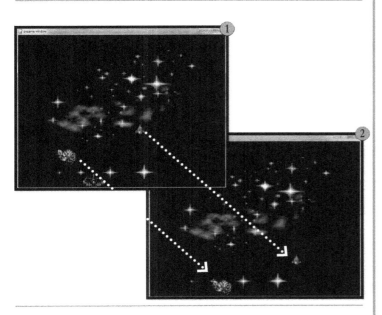

Figure 3-2: *enemy* and *asteroid* are both moving off the screen along with *player*.

14 In the game loop in main.py modify the "Update game state" section so that it contains a **for in** loop instead of a single call to *player.update()*. This is shown in code example 3-11.

15 In order to verify that the updates are being called, modify the acceleration values of the Asteroid and Enemy classes to 0.1 and run the program. You should see every game object except for *background* slowly moving off of the screen.

16 Once you've verified that the updates are being performed, reset the acceleration and velocity values of the Enemy and Asteroid classes.

```
import pygame
from imageLoader import *

class Player(pygame.sprite.Sprite):
    def __init__(self, image, scale, clip, ckey):
        self.image = imageLoader(image, scale, clip)
        self.image.set_colorkey(ckey)
        self.rect = self.image.get_rect()
        self.rect.x = 400
        self.rect.y = 300
        self.velocityX = 0
        self.velocityY = 0
        self.accelerationX = 0.1
        self.accelerationY = 0.1

    def update(self):
        #Process player input
        #Collision detection
        #Update physics
        self.velocityX += self.accelerationX
        self.velocityY += self.accelerationY
        self.rect.x += self.velocityX
        self.rect.y += self.velocityY

class Enemy(pygame.sprite.Sprite):
    def __init__(self, image, scale, clip, ckey):
        self.image = imageLoader(image, scale, clip)
        self.image.set_colorkey(ckey)
        self.rect = self.image.get_rect()
        self.rect.x = 200
        self.rect.y = 100
        self.velocityX = 0
        self.velocityY = 0
        self.accelerationX = 0
        self.accelerationY = 0

    def update(self):
        self.velocityX += self.accelerationX
        self.velocityY += self.accelerationY
        self.rect.x += self.velocityX
        self.rect.y += self.velocityY
```

```
class Asteroid(pygame.sprite.Sprite):
    def __init__(self, image, scale, clip, ckey):
     self.image = imageLoader(image, scale, clip)
     self.image.set_colorkey(ckey)
     self.rect = self.image.get_rect()
     self.rect.x = 100
     self.rect.y = 400
     self.velocityX = 0
     self.velocityY = 0
     self.accelerationX = 0
     self.accelerationY = 0

    def update(self):
     self.velocityX += self.accelerationX
     self.velocityY += self.accelerationY
     self.rect.x += self.velocityX
     self.rect.y += self.velocityY

class Background(pygame.sprite.Sprite):
    def __init__(self, image, width, height):
     self.originalAsset = pygame.image.load(image)
     self.image = pygame.transform.scale(self.originalAsset, (width,height) )
     self.rect = self.image.get_rect()
    def update(self):
     return
```

Example 3-12: The complete gameObjects.py code

In this section we have implemented some very basic physics, but the core of a more complex game physics system is in place. We are performing small movements of our objects every time the game loop iterates and we are setting the rules that govern those movements.

So far, we have learned how to use a set, constant speed and we have also learned how to implement acceleration. In the next section we will expand our physics system to include player control and ship rotation. We will also organize the code in our Player class to make it more readable and easier to maintain.

As we work on implementing physics, take time to experiment with different values to gain a better understanding of how your physics engine affects the way that your game feels. Use the code examples as a guide, but fine tune the values to create gameplay that feels right to you.

Questions for Review:

1 What do Pong and Star Citizen have in common?

    a They both involve spaceships.

    b Both games will play on an Atari.

    c Both games are simulations that use a physics engine.

    d They both feature a stout Italian plumber as a main character.

2 What is the simplest way to create movement in a 2D game?

    a Create an accurate simulation of subatomic particles and work out from there.

    b Change the x and y coordinates of objects in every frame.

    c Keep the objects to be moved static, but change the x and y coordinates of every other object in the game every frame.

    d You cannot represent movement in a 2D game, you need a 3D game.

3 Why is it useful to use acceleration?

    a To increase velocity in every loop iteration.

    b Acceleration is not useful.

    c To give players control of velocity.

    d To reduce the processing overhead of the physics engine.

4 The update() method of our objects is intended to hold all of the code that we want updated in each frame.

    a True.

    b False.

3.2 Player Input

In the previous section, we introduced very simple physics into our game. In this section, we will expand on the physics system by introducing player input.

First, we need to consider what we intend to achieve in our game. We are working on an overhead space action game, so we want our player to be able to move in any direction. To keep things simple, we will use the arrow keys as the input method and we will simplify the rotation to only cover eight possible angles.

In chapter one we included player input directly in the game loop, however, in this case, we are going to process our player input in the Player class. Also, we are going to include code to handle the rotation of the player object and process increasingly complicated physics. All of this processing has to occur as a part of the update method, but we do not want to include it all in the update method. Instead, we will create additional methods in the Player class to perform functions like physics updates, player input processing, and ship rotation.

The three methods that we are going to create are *Player.updatePhysics()*, *Player. getPlayerInput()*, and *Player.processControl()*. The first two are self explanatory, but the last new method, *Player.processControl()*, is where we will handle ship rotation and directional movement. Open up gameObject.py and get ready to write some code!

1 Create the three new methods in your Player class.

2 In *Player.update()*, call the new methods. First in the "Process player input" section, call *self.getPlayerInput()* and *self.processControl()*. Next, in the "Update physics section" call *self.updatePhysics()*. Example 3-13 shows this code.

```
def update(self):
    #Process player input
    self.getPlayerInput()
    self.processControl()
    #Collision Detection
    #Update physics
    self.updatePhysics()
def updatePhysics(self):
def getPlayerInput(self):
def processControls(self):
```

Example 3-13: New methods and updated update.

```
def updatePhysics(self):
    self.velocityX += self.accelerationX
    self.velocityY += self.accelerationY
    self.rect.x += self.velocityX
    self.rect.y += self.velocityY
```

Example 3-14: Put the physics updates into *Player.updatePhysics()*.

```
def getPlayerInput(self):
    up = pygame.key.get_pressed()[pyg-
ame.K_UP]
    right = pygame.key.get_pressed()[pyg-
ame.K_RIGHT]
    down = pygame.key.get_pressed()[pyg-
ame.K_DOWN]
    left = pygame.key.get_pressed()[pyg-
ame.K_LEFT]
    return up,right,down,left
```

Example 3-15: Use **pygame.key.get_pressed()** to capture key presses in *Player.getPlayerInput()*.

```
def update(self):
    #Process player input
    controls = self.getPlayerInput()
    self.processControls()
    #Collision Detection
    #Update physics
    self.updatePhysics()
```

Example 3-16: Save the player input into *control* during each game loop iteration with *Player.update()*.

3 The first thing that we are going to do is put the physics that we created in section 3.1 into *Player.updatePhysics()*, shown in example 3-14.

4 Now we are going to capture the player's input. In *Player.getPlayerInput()* define variables for up, down, left, and right and set them to the Boolean value of the appropriate key presses. Have the method return those values, as shown in example 3-15.

Now we have a method that returns an array, which contains Booleans for the arrow keys, and with the True value for those that are being pressed. This array gives us something to process in *Player.processControl()*.

5 In *Player.update()*, create a variable named *control* and assign it the array returned from *Player.getPlayerInput()*, as shown in example 3-16.

6 *Player.processControls()* is going to be the method that processes player inputs, so modify *Player.update()* to pass *controls* to *Player.processControls()*, as in example 3-17.

```
def update(self):
    #Process player input
    controls = self.getPlayerInput()
    self.processControls(controls)
    #Collision Detection
    #Update physics
    self.updatePhysics()
```

Example 3-17: Update *Player.update()* to pass *controls* to *Player.processControls()*.

7 Now that we know that *Player.processControls()* will take an argument, example 3-18 shows how to modify the method declaration to take the appropriate parameter.

```
def processControls(self, control):
```

Example 3-18: Modify the definition of *Player.processControls()* to take *controls* as a parameter.

8 In the body of *Player.processControl()* we are going to use a series of conditionals to determine the direction of the Player object. Our *controls* array has the directions up, right, down, and left in locations 0, 1, 2, and 3. This means that if *control[0]* is true, then the player is pressing the up arrow key, and therefore we want the Player object to move negatively along the Y axis. Understanding that, example 3-19 shows the resulting player control code. Note that we first check for combinations of keys, and then allow the **if elif** to fall through to check individual keys.

```
if control[0] and control[1]:
    #Player pressed Up/Right
elif control[0] and control[3]:
    #Player pressed Up/Left
elif control[2] and control[1]:
    #Player pressed Down/Right
elif control[2] and control[3]:
    #Player pressed Down/Left
elif control[0]:
    #Player pressed Up
elif control[1]:
    #Player pressed Right
elif control[2]:
    #Player pressed Down
elif control[3]:
    #Player pressed Left
```

Example 3-19: Parsing the player input according to which keys were pressed.

```
if control[0] and control[1]:
    self.velocityY = -1
    self.velocityX = 1
elif control[0] and control[3]:
    self.velocityY = -1
    self.velocityX = -1
elif control[2] and control[1]:
    self.velocityY = 1
    self.velocityX = 1
elif control[2] and control[3]:
    self.velocityY = 1
    self.velocityX = 1
elif control[0]:
    self.velocityY = -1
    self.velocityX = 0
elif control[1]:
    self.velocityX = 1
    self.velocityY = 0
elif control[2]:
    self.velocityY = 1
    self.velocityX = 0
elif control[3]:
    self.velocityY = 0
    self.velocityX = -1
else:
    self.velocityX = 0
    self.velocityY = 0
```

Example 3-20: The code to move the player's ship.

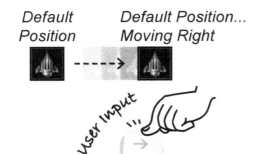

Default Position Default Position...
                  Moving Right

User Input

Figure 3-3: Now the ship moves with the arrow keys!

9 Before we implement rotation, we are going to ensure that the player's ship will move. Replace the comments in *Player.processControls()* with code to assign either 1 or -1 to the values of *self.velocityX* and *self.velocityY,* depending on the direction the ship should move. Example 3-20 demonstrates this. Note that we have added an **else** statement to set the velocities to 0. This ensures that the player ship will stop when no key is being pressed.

You have probably noticed that we are using a set value for our velocity. Our acceleration values are not being used in this case because we are specifically setting the values of our velocity variables in each iteration of the game loop. We will fix this later. First, we will implement rotation so our ship faces the direction that it is traveling.

We are going to use **pygame.transform.rotate()** to implement rotation, but we are not going to use the transform operation directly on *self.image*. Instead, we will create *self.asset* to store the unmodified version of our asset and then store a rotated version of *self.asset* as *self.image*. We are doing this because we want to apply a set rotation to an image that we can be certain has no rotation. If we applied the rotation to an already rotated *self.image* in each iteration of the game loop, then our player's space ship would spin wildly whenever any key was pressed.

We also need to consider how Pygame handles rotation. The **pygame.transform. rotate()** method returns a new surface that is based on a rotated version of the surface object it was passed. Surface objects are always rectangular, so a surface that has been rotated to any angle other than 90 degrees will always return a surface with a larger area than the original. If that surface is then rotated again, as would happen if we only used *self.image*, the resulting surface would continue growing until the program crashes. By only ever applying a rotate operation to *self.asset* and only ever displaying *self.image*, we avoid that problem.

```
self.asset = imageLoader(image, scale,
  clip)
self.image = self.asset
```

Example 3-21: Modify the Player class constructor.

10 First, in the Player class constructor, set the loaded image to *self.asset* instead of *self.image*, and then set *self.image* to *self. asset.* Code example 3-21 shows what the code should look like.

```
self.angle = 0
```

Example 3-22: Set the default angle to 0 degrees.

11 Next, set up an angle attribute in the Player class constructor and initialize it to 0, as shown in example 3-22.

```
self.image = pygame.transform.rotate(-
  self.asset, self.angle)
```

Example 3-23: Perform the rotation in *Player.update()*..

```
def processControls(self, control):
    if control[0] and control[3]:
        self.angle = 45
        self.velocityY = -1
        self.velocityX = -1
    elif control[0] and control[1]:
        self.angle = 315
        self.velocityY = -1
        self.velocityX = 1
    elif control[1] and control[2]:
        self.angle = 225
        self.velocityY = 1
        self.velocityX = 1
    elif control[2] and control[3]:
        self.angle = 135
        self.velocityY = 1
        self.velocityX = -1
    elif control[0]:
        self.angle = 0
        self.velocityY = -1
        self.velocityX = 0
    elif control[1]:
        self.angle = 270
        self.velocityY = 0
        self.velocityX = 1
    elif control[2]:
        self.angle = 180
        self.velocityY = 1
        self.velocityX = 0
    elif control[3]:
        self.velocityY = 0
        self.velocityX = -1
        self.angle = 90
    else:
        self.velocityY = 0
        self.velocityX = 0
```

Example 3-24: In *Player.processControls()*, determine the appropriate rotation angle according to the keys the player has pressed.

12 Then, in *Player.update()*, set *self.image* to the result of *self.asset* being rotated *self.angle* degrees, as in example 3-23 on the previous page. When the game loads, *self.angle* will be 0, so the ship will be facing up.

13 Finally, in the body of *Player.processControl()*, for each of the eight possible directions the ship can be facing set *self.angle* to the appropriate value in degrees, from 0 to 315, in steps of 45. Code example 3-24 shows what *Player.processControl()* should look like.

Now when you run the game you'll see the player ship moving and rotating in the direction that it's moving! Your game is coming along, but it doesn't yet feel like a space game should, and the movement is very sluggish. We'll fix that slow movement next.

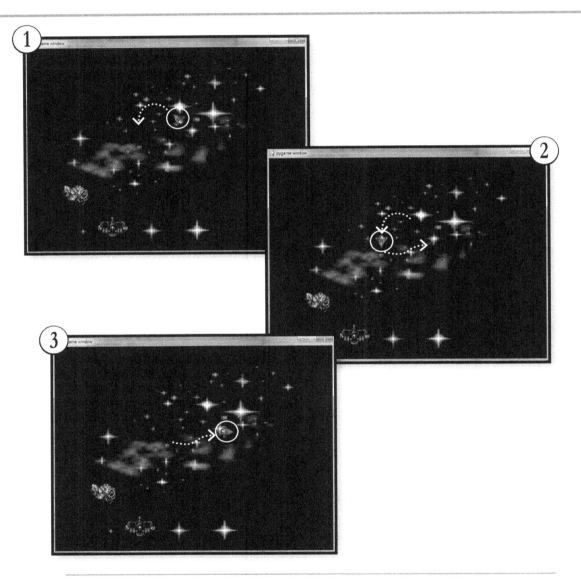

Figure 3-4: Ship rotation now matches the direction of movement.

```
▸   self.speed = 5
```

Example 3-25: Set a speed in the Player class constructor.

```
▸   self.rect.x += self.velocityX * self.
    speed
▸   self.rect.y += self.velocityY * self.
    speed
```

Example 3-26: Multiply the velocity by the speed to make the ship move faster.

---

14 The simplest way to increase the speed of the Player object is simply to add a *self.speed* attribute. Create it in the Player class constructor, shown in example 3-25.

15 In *Player.updatePhysics()*, multiply the value of *self.velocityX* and *self.velocityY* with the *self.speed*, as in example 3-26.

Now the ship is moving much faster and the game feels very snappy. That's definitely an improvement, but the game still doesn't feel the way that a space game should feel. There is no sense of inertia that one might expect from an object moving in space.

In the next section, we will implement movement based on thrust and damping to make the player's ship move in a more appropriate manner. The ship will have a sense of inertia and will slide around as it moves.

WHAT HAVE YOU LEARNED?

Questions for Review:

1 What is the first thing to consider when creating player input?

    a How easy it will be to implement.

    b Which controller we want people to use.

    c What we want our player to be able to do.

    d What method we will use for the player input code.

2 How do we use the values returned from pygame.key.get_pressed()?

    a We don't.

    b Store them as an attribute.

    c Store them in an array to be processed later.

    d Use them to set the acceleration attribute.

3 What does pygame.transform.rotate() return?

    a A new surface scaled to fit the rotated source surface.

    b Nothing.

    c It modifies the source surface and returns a Boolean True if the rotation was successful, and False if it was not.

    d A surface of the same size as the source with the source cropped to fit.

4 There is no need to maintain an unmodified version of a rotated game asset.

    a True.

    b False.

3.3 Thrust and Damping

In this section, we will continue with our physics system to introduce thrust and damping as a means of controlling the player's ship and as a way to introduce more interesting, realistic gameplay.

Open up your gameObjects.py and main.py files. We will be primarily working on the Player class gameObjects.py.

```
self.thrust = 0.5
```

Example 3-27: Change *self.speed* to *self.thrust* and give it a low value.

```
if control[0] and control[3]:
    self.angle = 45
elif control[0] and control[1]:
    self.angle = 315
elif control[1] and control[2]:
    self.angle = 225
elif control[2] and control[3]:
    self.angle = 135
elif control[0]:
    self.angle = 0
elif control[1]:
    self.angle = 270
elif control[2]:
    self.angle = 180
elif control[3]:
    self.angle = 90
```

Example 3-28: Clear out the references to *self.velocityX* and *self.velocityY* in *Player.processControl()*.

1 First, change the *self. speed* attribute in the Player class constructor to *self.thrust*. Set the value of *self.thrust* to a small number. like 0.5. This is shown in example 3-27.

2 In *Player.update()* remove the references to *self.speed*.

3 In *Player.processControl()* there is a lot of duplicate code. We are going to use thrust to control our ship instead of a set velocity, so remove all of the code that sets the values of *self. velocityX* and *self.velocityY*. *Player.processControl()* should look like example 3-28. Note that we no longer need the final **else** statement.

Thrust is a reaction force that accelerates a system in the opposite direction of mass that has been expelled from that system. Think about the way rockets work: fuel is combusted and expelled out of the base of a rocket and the force of that expulsion causes the rocket to accelerate. In our simple physics engine the *self.thrust* attribute represents the power of that rocket.

We will use *self.thrust* and some math to determine which direction the player's ship should accelerate. For now, we will only consider movement on the X axis. If we want our ship to move to the right, then we need to affect a positive change to the X coordinate, and if we want it to move to the left, then we need to affect a negative change to the X coordinate. Those changes can be made by multiplying our X axis velocity by 1 or -1, with 1 representing movement to the right, and -1 representing movement to the left.

We have set the values of every button press to be stored as Booleans, which are either 1 or 0. If the right arrow key being pressed is true then *control[1]* has a Boolean value of 1, which would represent movement to the right. However, the left arrow key, *control[3]*, being pressed also returns a Boolean value of 1, which still represents movement to the right.

In order to get a value of -1, representing movement to the left, when the left arrow key is pressed, we need to subtract the value of *control[3]*, which would be 1, from 0. We know that when the right arrow key is *not* pressed, *control[1]* has a Boolean value of 0, so if we subtract *control[3]* when the left arrow key *is* being pressed from *control[1]* when the right arrow key *is not* being pressed we are subtracting 1 from 0, resulting in -1 which represents movement to the left. Similarly, if only the right arrow key is being pressed then *control[1]* would be 1 and *control[3]* would be 0, so the same equation would result in 1, which represents movement to the right.

In this way, we can determine which direction to apply thrust by multiplying *self.thrust* by the value of *control[1]* minus *control[3]*. The same equation works for movement on the Y axis, only we need to multiply *self.thrust* by the value of *control[2]* minus *control[0]* because the origin point of the Y axis is on the top of *screen*.

Once we know the direction of acceleration on the X and Y axes, we can assign that value to *self.accelerationX* and *self.accelerationY*. In *Player.updatePhysics()*, the acceleration attributes are used to calculate the ship's velocity. In this way, modifying the *self.thrust* attribute will change how the ship moves.

4 In *Player.processControl()* add code that calculates *self.accelerationX* and *self.accelerationY*, as in example 3-29. Refer to figure 3-5 if you are having trouble understanding why this code works.

```
self.accelerationX = self.thrust * (control[1] - control[2])
self.accelerationY = self.thrust * (control[2] - control[0])
```

Example 3-29: Setting acceleration using thrust and direction.

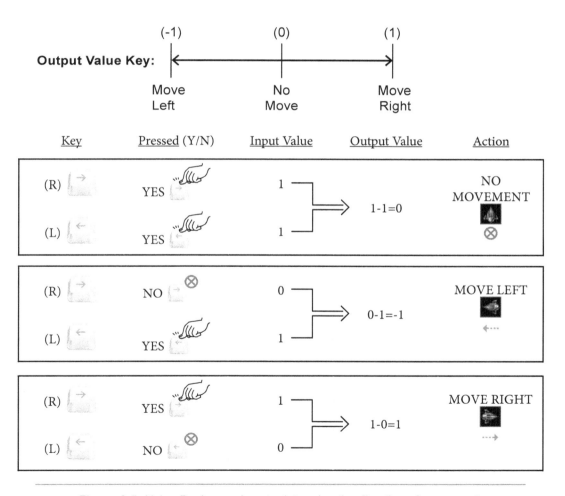

Figure 3-5: Using Boolean values to determine the direction of movement.

Run the game to test the changes. Your player's ship is now controlled by thrust! It's beginning to move how we imagine a space ship actually should move. Excellent! Of course, as it is, you probably find it pretty easy to launch the ship out of the viewable area. This is because there is no force acting against the motion of the ship. To slow the ship down, we are going to implement a damping force that counteracts the thrust force that we have just applied. This will make the ship gradually slow to a stop when the player takes their finger off of the arrow keys. We are going to apply damping in *Player.updatePhysics()* and also create a damping attribute in the Player class constructor.

5 First, prepare the attribute. In the Player class constructor, create *self.damping* and set it to a number lower than the value of *self.thrust*. It is important that damping is lower than thrust because if the force acting to stop the ship (damping) is higher than the force acting to move the ship (thrust) then the ship will not move. Refer to example 3-30.

```
self.thrust = 0.5
self.damping = 0.3
```

Example 3-30: In the Player class constructor, create *self.damping* and ensure that it is lower than *self.thrust*.

6 In *Player.updatePhysics()*, enter the code in example 3-31. Although there is only one damping value, we need to apply damping separately to the X and Y axes. We are removing the value of *self.damping* from *velocityX* and *velocityY* during each game loop iteration. If the velocity is already lower than *self.damping,* we stop the ship.

```
#Apply damping horizontal
if self.velocityX < 0 - self.damping:
    self.velocityX += self.damping
if self.velocityX > 0 + self.damping:
    self.velocityX -= self.damping:
else:
    self.velocityX = 0

#Apply damping vertical
if self.velocityY < 0 - self.damping:
    self.velocityY += self.damping
if self.velocityY > 0 + self.damping:
    self.velocityY -= self.damping
else:
    self.velocityY = 0
```

Example 3-31: In *Player.updatePhysics()* implement damping by slowing the velocity by the value of *self.damping* in both directions on both axes.

Run the game and see how the ship's movement feels now. Much better! The ship will slow down and stop when no keys are being pressed. To get a better feel for how thrust and damping effect gameplay, modify the values of both attributes and run the game again. Remember, the values we use in the book are not set in stone. Experimentation is the best way to understand how game mechanics work.

There is one more component that we are going to add to our Player class: maximum velocity. Like damping, to implement a maximum speed we will add an attribute in the class constructor and some code to *Player.updatePhysics()*.

```
self.maxVelocity = 8
```

Example 3-32: Set the maximum speed you want the player's ship to be able to travel.

7 First, in the Player class constructor, create *self.maxVelocity* and set it to a reasonable value, as in example 3-32.

```
#Cap max velocity
if self.velocityX > self.maxVelocity:
    self.velocityX = self.maxVelocity
if self.velocityX < self.maxVelocity *
-1:
    self.velocityX = self.maxVelocity *
-1
if self.velocityY > self.maxVelocity:
    self.velocityY = self.maxVelocity
if self.velocityY < self.maxVelocity *
-1:
    self.velocityY = self.maxVelocity *
-1
```

Example 3-33: In *Player.updatePhysics()* ensure that the player ship's velocity does not exceed *self.maxVelocity*.

8 In *Player.updatePhysics()*, check if the player's ship is moving higher than *self.maxVelocity* in any direction and, if so, set its velocity back to the value of *self.maxVelocity*. Remember that movement to the left and movement up are represented by negative velocities. The code in *Player.updatePhysics()* is shown in example 3-33.

```
class Player(pygame.sprite.Sprite):
    def __init__(self, image, scale, clip, ckey):
            self.asset = imageLoader(image, scale, clip)
            self.image = self.asset
            self.image.set_colorkey(ckey)
            self.rect = self.image.get_rect()
            self.rect.x = 400
            self.rect.y = 300
            self.velocityX = 0
            self.maxVelocity = 8
            self.accelerationX = 0
            self.accelerationY = 0
            self.thrust = .5
            self.damping = 0.3
            self.angle = 0

    def update(self):
            #Process player input
            controls = self.getPlayerInput()
            self.processControl(controls)
            self.image = pygame.transform.rotate(self.asset, self.angle)

            #Collision Detection

            #Update physics
            self.updatePhysics()
```

```
def updatePhysics(self):
        self.velocityX += self.accelerationX
        self.velocityY += self.accelerationY

        #Apply damping horizontal
        if self.velocityX < 0 - self.damping:
                self.velocityX += self.damping
        elif self.velocityX > 0 + self.damping:
                self.velocityX -= self.damping
        else:
                self.velocityX = 0
        #Apply damping vertical
        if self.velocityY < 0 - self.damping:
                self.velocityY += self.damping
        elif self.velocityY > 0 + self.damping:
                self.velocityY -= self.damping
        else:
                self.velocityY = 0

        #Cap max velocity
                if self.velocityX > self.maxVelocity:
        self.velocityX = self.maxVelocity
        if self.velocityX < self.maxVelocity * -1:
                self.velocityX = self.maxVelocity * -1
        if self.velocityY > self.maxVelocity:
                self.velocityY = self.maxVelocity
        if self.velocityY < self.maxVelocity * -1:
                self.velocityY = self.maxVelocity * -1

        #Set new position
        self.rect.x += self.velocityX
        self.rect.y += self.velocityY
```

```
def getPlayerInput(self):
        up = pygame.key.get_pressed()[pygame.K_UP]
        right = pygame.key.get_pressed()[pygame.K_RIGHT]
        down = pygame.key.get_pressed()[pygame.K_DOWN]
        left = pygame.key.get_pressed()[pygame.K_LEFT]
        return up,right,down,left

def processControl(self, control):
        if control[0] and control[3]:
                self.angle = 45
        elif control[0] and control[1]:
                self.angle = 315
        elif control[1] and control[2]:
                self.angle = 225
        elif control[2] and control[3]:
                self.angle = 135
        elif control[0]:
                self.angle = 0
        elif control[1]:
                self.angle = 270
        elif control[2]:
                self.angle = 180
        elif control[3]:
                self.angle = 90

        self.accelerationX = self.thrust * (control[1] - control[3])
        self.accelerationY = self.thrust * (control[2] - control[0])
```

Example 3-34: The complete Player class in gameObjects.py

Congratulations, you've completed the player ship's physics! Now is a good time to continue experimenting with different values for thrust, damping, and maximum speed to create a game that feels the way you like.

If you're not entirely clear how some of the concepts introduced in this chapter work, then simplify the code by considering movement along only a single axis. Work through the implementations of thrust, damping, and player movement until you understand how they work in a linear environment, and then consider how adding the second axis will effect an object's position. Every game you create, whether it's a fantastically elaborate space epic with precisely modeled gravity, or a simple endless runner where the only input a player has is to press "jump", will require you to understand motion. Taking the time now to grasp the basic concepts of game physics will make your life as a game developer easier.

Our ship can move around the screen, but it can't currently collide or interact with anything else. We'll fix that in the next section when we introduce some basic collision detection.

WHAT HAVE YOU LEARNED?

Questions for Review:

1 What is thrust?

a A new type of energy drink.

b Another word for "acceleration."

c A way to represent velocity in a 2D game.

d A reaction force that accelerates a system.

2 What does our damping force do?

a Counteracts the thrust force.

b Slows down the player's ship.

c Ensures that the player stops when no key is being pressed.

d All of the above.

3 There is no good reason to modify the values of thrust and damping used in this chapter.

a True.

b False.

4 The best way to create a gameplay experience that matches your goals is through experimentation and testing.

a True.

b False.

3.4 Collision Detection

In this section, we will introduce some simple collision detection into our space game. There are many degrees of granularity and methods of implementation for collision detection, but the basic premise is simple. Collision detection is determining if an object in your game is in contact with another object.

Collision detection can occur on anything from a per-pixel level, where each individual pixel that represents a game element is checked for contact, up to large boxes that enclose the game element. These boxes, called bounding boxes or hitboxes, are often used because they are less resource intensive than more precise methods.

It is common practice to only check for collisions between relevant objects. In our game, for example, we are not concerned if the player ship can collide with the background, so we will not check the background for collisions.

We will use object surface rectangles for collision detection in our game.

> **Collision detection**
>
> Collision detection is determining if an object in your game is in contact with another object.

```
self.collision = False
self.collisionGroup = []
```

Example 3-35: In the Player class constructor of gameObjects.py, add attributes to handle collisions.

1. The first thing that we will do is prepare the Player class constructor. Create *self. collision* and initialize it to False and then create an empty array *self.collisionGroup*. That array will store references to the objects that a Player object can collide with. Figure 3-35 shows the new code.

Now that we have an attribute that stores if a Player object has collided, and an attribute to store what a Player object can collide with, we have to create some code to actually check for collisions.

2 We want to check for collisions every time a Player object is updated, so create a *Player.checkForCollisions()* method and call it in *Player. update()*. This is shown in code examples 3-36 and 3-37.

3 Within *Player. checkForCollisions()* we will call the **pygame.rect.colliderect()** method for *self.rect* to determine if there is a collision. *self.rect. colliderect()* takes a rect as an argument and returns a Boolean True if any portion of either rectangle overlaps.

We use *self.rect.colliderect()* in a **for in** loop that will check every game object that is a part of the Player object's *collisionGroup*. If there is a collision, then we break out of the loop.

```
def update(self):
    #Process player input
    controls = self.getPlayerInput()
    self.processControl(controls)
    self.image = pygame.transform.ro-
tate(self.asset, self.angle)

    #Collision detection
    self.checkForCollisions()

    #Update physics
    self.updatePhysics()
```

Example 3-36: Setting up *Player.checkForCollisions()* in *Player. update()*

```
def checkForCollisions(self):
```

Example 3-37: Defining *Player.checkForCollisions()* in the Player class.

```
for gameObject in self.collisionGroup:
    self.collision = self.rect.collid-
erect(gameObject.rect)
    if self.collision: break
```

Example 3-38: The body of *Player.checkForCollisions()* uses pygame's **pygame.rectcolliderect()** method to check collisions.

We now have a Player object that contains an attribute to determine if it is colliding with something, has a list of objects that it can collide with, and that has logic to determine whether or not a collision has occurred. We are done with gameObjects.py for now.

In main.py we will add objects that a Player object can collide with to *Player. collisionGroup* and then we will have *screen* fill with red when a collision occurs. Ensure that you are working on main.py now.

4 First, outside of the game loop and after the game objects have been created, append *enemy* and *asteroid* to *player.collisionGroup*, as in example 3-39.

```
#Set collision groups
player.collisionGroup.append(enemy)
player.collisionGroup.append(asteroid)
```

Example 3-39: In main.py, add *enemy* and *asteroid* to the *player.collisionGroup* array.

When *player* collides with *enemy* or *asteroid,* we want the screen to turn red, but we also want the game objects to remain visible. To do this, we need to either draw *background* or fill *screen* and then draw the game objects.

```
#Display game updates
if player.collision:
    screen.fill( (255,0,0) )
else:
    screen.blit(background.image, (back-
ground.rect.x, background.rect.y) )
for gameObject in gameObjects:
    screen.blit(gameObject.image, (gameO-
bject.rect.x, gameObject.rect.y) )
pygame.display.flip()
```

Example 3-40: Render the screen depending on whether or not there is a collision, and then render the game objects on top.

5 Modify your code so that *background* is no longer included in *gameObjects.*

6 In the game loop, create a conditional to evaluate *player.collision* and fill *screen* with red if it's true or display *background* if it's false, as shown in example 3-40.

Now, when you collide with *enemy* you will see the display flash red, as in figure 3-6. The display will also flash red when you collide with *asteroid*, as in figure 3-7.

Move around *asteroid* and *enemy* and get a feel for where the actual collisions occur. You can clearly determine that the hitboxes for all objects are well beyond the actual pixels that define the object's graphics. Figure 3-8 shows the objects not appearing to collide even though *screen* is fully red.

This is the problem with using hitboxes — imprecision. You can mitigate this problem by creating additional rects to act as hitboxes and giving them different sizes or by creating a pixel-accurate collision detection system, but you will need more system resources as your collision detection becomes more complicated and precise.

Game development involves compromise. Collision detection is an area where great game developers find the best balance between creating gameplay that feels good and maximizing use of system resources.

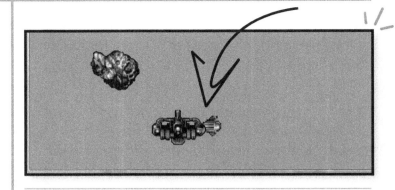

Figure 3-6: *player* colliding with *enemy*.

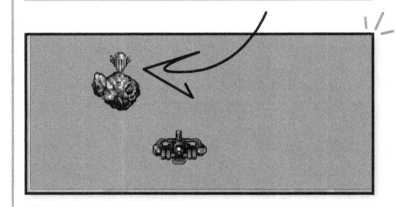

Figure 3-7: *player* colliding with *asteroid*

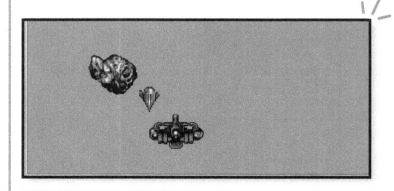

Figure 3-8: *player* colliding with seemingly nothing.

```
# Game Loop Template
import pygame, sys
from gameObjects import *

pygame.init()

#Create the application window
screen = pygame.display.set_mode( (800,600) )

#Create the game objects
background = Background("images/Nebula1.bmp", screen.get_width(), screen.
get_height())
player = Player("images/Hunter1.bmp", 2, (25,1,23,23), (0,0,0) )
enemy = Enemy("images/SpacStor.bmp", 1, (101,13,91,59), (69,78,91) )
asteroid = Asteroid("images/Rock2a.bmp", 1, (6,3,80,67), (69,78,91) )

#Set collision groups
player.collisionGroup.append(enemy)
player.collisionGroup.append(asteroid)

#Create the game objects collection
gameObjects = []
gameObjects.append(player)
gameObjects.append(enemy)
gameObjects.append(asteroid)

#Create the game clock
clock = pygame.time.Clock()
```

```
#The game loop
while True:
    for event in pygame.event.get():
        if event.type == pygame.QUIT :
            pygame.quit()

    #Update the game state
    for gameObject in gameObjects:
     gameObject.update()

    #Display the game updates
    if player.collision:
     screen.fill( (255,0,0) )
    else:
     screen.blit(background.image, (background.rect.x, background.rect.y) )
    for gameObject in gameObjects:
     screen.blit(gameObject.image, (gameObject.rect.x, gameObject.rect.y) )
    pygame.display.flip()
    clock.tick(60)
```

Example 3-41: The complete main.py

```
import pygame
from imageLoader import *

class Background(pygame.sprite.Sprite):
    def __init__(self, image, width, height):
     self.originalAsset = pygame.image.load(image)
     self.image = pygame.transform.scale(self.originalAsset, (width,height))
     self.rect = self.image.get_rect()
    def update(self)
     return

class Player(pygame.sprite.Sprite):
    def __init__(self, image, scale, clip, ckey):
     self.asset = imageLoader(image, scale, clip)
     self.image = self.asset
     self.image.set_colorkey(ckey)
     self.rect = self.image.get_rect()
     self.rect.x = 400
     self.rect.y = 300
     self.velocityX = 0
     self.velocityY = 0
     self.maxVelocity = 8
     self.accelerationX = 0
     self.accelerationY = 0
     self.thrust = 0.5
     self.damping = 0.3
     self.angle = 0
     self.collision = False
     self.collisionGroup = []

    def update(self)
     #Process player input
     controls = self.getPlayerInput()
     self.processControl(controls)
     self.image = pygame.transform.rotate(self.asset, self.angle)
     #Collision Detection
     self.checkForCollisions()
     #Update physics
     self.updatePhysics()
```

```
def checkForCollisions(self):
  for gameObject in self.collisionGroup:
        self.collision = self.rect.colliderect(gameObject.rect)
        if self.collision: break

def updatePhysics(self):
  self.velocityX += self.accelerationX
  self.velocityY += self.accelerationY

  #Apply damping horizontal
  if self.velocityX < 0 - self.damping:
        self.velocityX += self.damping
  elif self.velocityY > 0 + self.damping:
        self.velocityX -= self.damping
  else:
        self.velocityX = 0
  #Apply damping vertical
  if self.velocityY < 0 - self.damping:
        self.velocityY += self.damping
  elif self.velocityY > 0 + self.damping:
        self.velocityY -= self.damping
  else:
        self.velocityY = 0

  #Cap maximum velocity
  if self.velocityX > self.maxVelocity:
        self.velocityX = self.maxVelocity
  if self.velocityX < self.maxVelocity * -1:
        self.velocityX = self.maxVelocity * -1
  if self.velocityY > self.maxVelocity:
        self.velocityY = self.maxVelocity
  if self.velocityY < self.maxVelocity * -1:
        self.velocityY = self.maxVelocity *

  #Set new position
  self.rect.x += self.velocityX
  self.rect.y += self.velocityY
```

```
def getPlayerInput(self):
  up = pygame.key.get_pressed()[pygame.K_UP]
  right = pygame.key.get_pressed()[pygame.K_RIGHT]
  down = pygame.key.get_pressed()[pygame.K_DOWN]
  left = pygame.key.get_pressed()[pygame.K_LEFT]
  return up,right,down,left

def processControl(self, control):
  if control[0] and control[3]:
        self.angle = 45
  elif control[0] and control[1]:
        self.angle = 315
  elif control[1] and control[2]:
        self.angle = 225
  elif control[2] and control[3]:
        self.angle = 135
  elif control[0]:
        self.angle = 0
  elif control[1]:
        self.angle = 270
  elif control[2]:
        self.angle = 180
  elif control[3]:
        self.angle = 90
  self.accelerationX = self.thrust * ( control[1] - control[3] )
  self.accelerationY = self.thrust * ( control[2] - control[0] )

class Enemy(pygame.sprite.Sprite):
  def __init__(self, image, scale, clip, ckey):
    self.image = imageLoader(image, sclae, clip)
    self.image.set_colorkey(ckey)
    self.rect = self.image.get_rect()
    self.rect.x = 200
    self.rect.y = 500
    self.velocityX = 0
    self.velocityY = 0
    self.accelerationX = 0
    self.accelerationY = 0
```

```
    def update(self)
      self.velocityX += self.accelerationX
      self.velocityY += self.accelerationY
      self.rect.x += self.velocityX
      self.rect.y += self.velocityY

class Asteroid(pygame.sprite.Sprite):
    def __init__(self, image, scale, clip, ckey):
      self.image = imageLoader(image, sclae, clip)
      self.image.set_colorkey(ckey)
      self.rect = self.image.get_rect()
      self.rect.x = 200
      self.rect.y = 500
      self.velocityX = 0
      self.velocityY = 0
      self.accelerationX = 0
      self.accelerationY = 0
    def update(self)
      self.velocityX += self.accelerationX
      self.velocityY += self.accelerationY
      self.rect.x += self.velocityX
      self.rect.y += self.velocityY
```

Example 3-42: The complete gameObject.py

In this chapter, we learned about physics in games and we implemented a physics system for our space game. We captured and parsed player input in order to move the Player object, and we enhanced the simple physics system that we started with by adding thrust and damping. We also learned about collision detection, and integrated some simple hitboxes into our game.

In the next chapter, we will learn about event logic, the difference between game event logic and game object logic, and we will work on timing in our game logic in order to ensure that game events happen when they are supposed to.

Questions for Review:

1 What is collision detection?

a Mapping the exact pixel location of a collision between objects.

b Determining the attributes of pixels adjacent to a source pixel.

c Determining if an object is in contact with another object.

d Reacting to the collision of two objects.

2 What are the collision boxes that enclose a game element called?

a Collision box.

b Collider box.

c Bounded box.

d Bounding box.

3 More precise collision detection is more processor intensive.

a True.

b False.

4 Using hitboxes, or bounding boxes, is a very precise method of collision detection.

a True.

b False.

CHAPTER 03 LAB EXERCISE

A simple ball bouncing around the screen isn't that much fun. In this lab exercise you'll be making that example more interesting by adding gravity and initial velocities.

1 Create a ball:

a) Draw a circle.

b) Give it an initial position and velocity

c) Move the ball by updating its position.

d) Make it bounce off the sides of the screen.

2 Add gravity:

a) Gravity is a force that causes acceleration by always pulling on an object. Add a constant downward acceleration to the ball.

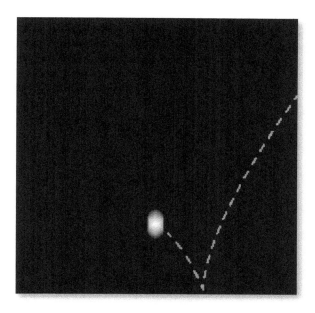

Exploring
Event Logic

Chapter Objectives:

- You will learn how to create logic for game objects.
- You will understand how to create logic for game events.
- You will learn how timing impacts gameplay.
- You will be able to implement delays and timed logic.

4.1 Game Object Logic

In this chapter, we're going to apply logic to the different game objects and trigger its execution based on events, instead of just the timer. First, we will create logic for game objects other than our player and then we will create event logic that only executes when certain game events have occurred.

Open up the main.py and gameObjects.py files. At the moment, our Player object can move around the screen and bump into instances of the Asteroid and Enemy objects. Although we have covered some of the most important hurdles in developing our game — creating a simple physics system and implementing a player movement system that feels appropriate — we still need to create obstacles and challenges for the player to overcome.

The first step to creating a more interesting game is going to be creating more Asteroid and Enemy objects, and then making those objects do something interesting. We will first focus on our Asteroid Class, by creating a scene where our player's ship is trying to avoid waves of asteroids hurtling through space.

In our simple game, we can add more Asteroid objects with a **for in** loop and appending the new Asteroid objects to the *gameObjects* array that we have created. Make sure that you're working in main.py, and follow along with these steps:

1 First, move the initialization of *gameObjects* so that it occurs prior to the creation of *enemy* and *asteroid*. You can then delete the code that appends *enemy* and *asteroid* to *gameObjects* and *player.collisionGroup*. Your "Create the game objects" code block should match example 4-1.

```
#Create the game objects
background = Background("images/
    Nebula1.bmp", screen.get_width(),
screen.get_height())
player = Player("images/hunter1.bmp", 2,
    (25,1,23,23), (0,0,0) )
gameObjects = []
gameObjects.append(player)
enemy = Enemy("images/SpaceEnemy.bmp", 1,
    (101,13,91,59), (69,78,91) )
asteroid = Asteroid("images/RockX2d.bmp",
    1, (6,3,80,67), (69,78,91) )
```

Example 4-1: Creating your game objects in main.py.

```
for i in range(5):
    asteroid = Asteroid("images/Rock2a.
    bmp", 1, (6,3,80,67), (69,78,91) )
    gameObjects.append(asteroid)
    player.collisionGroup.append(
asteroid)
```

Example 4-2: A **for in** loop to create Asteroid objects.

```
for i in range(3):
    enemy = Enemy("images/SpaceStar.bmp",
    1, (101,13,91,59), (69,78,91) )
    gameObjects.append(enemy)
    player.collisionGroup.append(enemy)
```

Example 4-3: A **for in** loop to create Enemy objects.

2 Now create a **for in** loop that contains the creation of *asteroid*. Within that loop, append *asteroid* to *gameObjects* and *player.collisionGroup*. This is shown in example 4-2.

3 Create the same type of **for in** loop for *enemy*, as shown in example 4-3. We have chosen to start with five Asteroid objects and three Enemy objects, but this may change as we test the game.

When you run the game you've probably noticed that everything looks exactly the same as it did before we modified our code. That's fine! What's happening is that each instance of the Enemy and Asteroid classes that you've created is being drawn to *screen* at the same coordiantes. Remember that they all have the same values for *self.rect.x* and *self.rect.y*. In order to position the new instances so that they are visible, we will have to modify the Classes and randomize the values of *self.rect.x* and *self.rect.y*.

Before we dive into gameObjects.py, we should consider what our new code is going to need. We will have to randomly position objects on *screen*, so we will want to know how large *screen* is. We have been using a static value for screen, 800 by 600, but that may not always be the case. Instead of passing the values "800" and "600" or hard-coding those values in gameObjects.py, we can modify main.py so that our desired screen size is a tuple and *screen* is created using that tuple. That way, when we need to pass the size of the application window to anything, we can just pass that tuple.

4 In your "Create the application window" code block in main.py, add a *screenXY* tuple with the values of 800 and 600, and then create *screen* with that tuple, as in example 4-4.

```
#Create the application window
screenXY = (800,600)
screen = pygame.display.set_
mode(screenXY)
```

Example 4-4: Creating *screen* using a tuple.

5 When you are creating Asteroid objects, pass *screenXY* as an argument, as shown in example 4-5.

```
for i in range(5):
    asteroid = Asteroid("images
Rock2a.bmp", 1, (6,3,80,67), (69,78,91),
screenXY )
    gameObjects.append(asteroid)
    player.collisionGroup.append
(asteroid)
```

Example 4-5: Passing *screenXY* as an argument to the Asteroid class constructor.

6 Now, in gameObjects.py, go to the Asteroid object and modify the constructor to accept the screen size tuple you have just created, as in example 4-6.

```
def __init__(self, image, scale, clip,
ckey, screenXY):
```

Example 4-6: Modifying the Asteroid Class constructor.

7 Create two additional attributes, *self.screenX* and *self.screenY*, to hold the dimensions of the application window and assign them the appropriate values from the tuple that you passed to the constructor. This is shown in example 4-7.

```
self.screenX = screenXY[0]
self.screenY = screenXY[1]
```

Example 4-7: Set screen size attributes.

8 We will position our Asteroid objects in a method called *Asteroid.reset()*. Create that method, shown in example 4-8.

```
def reset(self):
    return
```

Example 4-8: Define an empty reset method.

```
▸  self.screenX = screenXY[0]
▸  self.screenY = screenXY[1]
▸  self.reset()
```

Example 4-9: The final lines of the Asteroid constructor.

```
▸  import pygame, random
```

Example 4-10: Ensure that gameObjects.py imports random.

```
▸  def reset(self):
▸      self.rect.x = random.randrange(0,
    screenX)
▸      self.rect.y = random.randrange(0,
    screenY)
```

Example 4-11: in Asteroid.reset() position the object.

9 At the end of the Class constructor, call the *Asteroid. reset()* method to ensure that every Asteroid that is created will have a different position, shown in example 4-9.

10 At the start of gameObjects.py import the random library (as shown in example 4-10) so that we can use the **random. randrange()** method.

11 In the body of the *Asteroid.reset()* method, set the position of *self.rect.x* and *self.rect.y* using **random. randrange()** with the values of *self.screenX* and *self. screenY*, as in example 4-11.

12 Make sure that you have saved gameObjects.py and then return to main.py. Run the program a few times to verify that the new Asteroid objects are appearing randomly on the screen. Figure 4-1 shows how your screen may look.

Figure 4-1: Asteroids now appear in random locations!

Now that we have a collection of Asteroid objects appearing on the screen, we need to make them move. They are going to be basic obstacles for our player to avoid so we will not need complicated logic. All we will do is modify their position in the *Asteroid.update()* method to move them across the screen.

We have already given the Asteroid class velocity and acceleration attributes, but we will only be using the velocity attributes to move the asteroids because we will assume that the asteroids flying through space at our player all have a constant speed.

13 We have already included the logic needed to move our Asteroid object, so all we need to do is set an appropriate speed. Do that by modifying *self.velocityX* and *self.velocityY* in the Asteroid constructor. Example 4-12 verifies what you should have in *Asteroid. update()* and example 4-13 shows the pertinent part of the class constructor. Note that we still have acceleration attributes, but they are not affecting the object because they are set to 0.

```
def update(self):
    self.velocityX += self.accelerationX
    self.velocityY += self.accelerationY
    self.rect.x += self.velocityX
    self.rect.y += self.velocityY
```

Example 4-12: *Asteroid.update()* is ready to move the Asteroid objects.

```
self.velocityX = 6
self.velocityY = 6
self.accelerationX = 0
self.accelerationY = 0
```

Example 4-13: In the Asteroid constructor set a velocity.

14 Now our asteroids appear randomly and move off of the screen, but we want them to move *from* off screen and then across the play area. To do this, we just need to spawn them outside of the visible area of *screen*. Modify *Asteroid.reset()*, as shown in example 4-14.

```
def reset(self):
    self.rect.x = random.randrange(0,
    screenX) * -1
    self.rect.y = random.randrange(0,
    screenY) * -1
```

Example 4-14: To have the asteroids drawn off screen multiply their initial location by -1.

By multiplying the initial values of *Asteroid.rect.x* and *Asteroid.rect.y* by -1, we have set the initial positions of the Asteroid objects to be above and to the left of the viewable area.

The asteroids now move across the screen as we would like, but there is only one wave of them. To create multiple waves of asteroids, we will re-use the Asteroid objects by calling *Asteroid.reset()* to reset their position when they move outside of the visible area of *screen*. We will do this using *Asteroid.screenX*, *Asteroid.screenY*, and the built in Pygame rect attributes.

```
▹   if self.rect.x >= self.rect.width +
    self.screenX or self.rect.y >= self.
    rect.height + self.screenY:
▹       self.reset()
```

Example 4-15: Reset the Asteroid objects' positions when they are no longer visible.

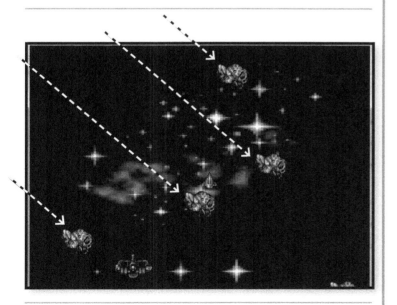

Figure 4-2: Our Asteroid objects now come in endless waves!

15 In *Asteroid.update()* create a conditional that checks if the value of *self.rect.x* is higher than the Asteroid object's own width, using *self.rect.width*, plus the known width of the screen, *self.screenX* OR if the value of *self.rect.y* is higher than the Asteroid object's own height plus the known height of the screen.

16 If either of the conditions in step 15 are true then the Asteroid object is off screen, so call *self.reset()* to reposition it, as shown in example 4-15.

We are reusing Asteroid objects like this because it can be computationally taxing to constantly create and destroy objects. It is much faster to reposition and reuse them.

```
class Asteroid(pygame.sprite.Sprite):
    def __init__(self, image, scale, clip, ckey, screenXY):
        self.image = imageLoader(image, scale, clip)
        self.image.set_colorkey(ckey)
        self.rect = self.image.get_rect()
        self.velocityX = 6
        self.velocityY = 6
        self.accelerationX = 0
        self.accelerationY = 0
        self.screenX = screenXY[0]
        self.screenY = screenXY[1]
        self.onSpawn()
    def update(self):
        self.velocityX += self.accelerationX
        self.velocityY += self.accelerationY
        self.rect.x += self.velocityX
        self.rect.y += self.velocityY
        if self.rect.x >= self.rect.width + self.screenX or self.rect.y >= self.
    rect.height + self.screenY:
            self.reset()
    def reset(self):
        self.rect.x = random.randrange(0,self.screenX) * -1
        self.rect.y = random.randrange(0,self.screenY) * -1
```

Example 4-16: The complete gameObject.py Asteroid class definition.

Our game is beginning to take shape. Asteroids now come at our player in endless waves, giving them interesting obstacles to avoid, and we have collision detection implemented so we can test to see if the player has been struck.

The logic attached to the Asteroid objects is object logic. In the next section, we will create logic that is executed when something specific happens, known as event logic.

Questions for Review:

1 What is game object logic?

a Game logic that controls certain game objects.

b All logic in the game.

c Code that is executed before the game loop begins.

d Code that is executed after the game loop ends.

2 Why do we call Asteroid. reset() at the end of the Asteroid class constructor?

a We do not call Asteroid. reset() at the end of the Asteroid class constructor.

b In order to reset the attributes of an Asteroid object to zero before it is used.

c In order to call the reset() method, the method that appropriately positions our Asteroid objects.

d Because the class constructor has to call all of the class methods.

3 Multiplying the positive x and y coordinates of an Asteroid object by -1 positions the object below and to the right of the game screen.

a True.

b False.

4 What is the best way to create endless waves of asteroid obstacles?

a Constantly create new Asteroid objects and ignore them after they move off screen.

b Constantly create new Asteroid objects, but destroy them when they move off screen.

c Reuse Asteroid objects by reversing their course when they move off screen.

d Reuse Asteroid objects by calling the Asteroid.reset() function when they move off screen.

4.2 Game Event Logic

Most game code is run every frame, but there are many situations where we want code to run only when a certain event occurs. That is where event logic comes into play.

We will create methods for all of our game objects called *onSpawn()*, *onDeath()*, and *reset()*. These three events — object spawning, object death, and object reset — will trigger specific code to be run.

1 First, create the method shells in the Player, Enemy, and Asteroid classes with code that matches example 4-17. Recall that *Asteroid.reset()* already exists.

```
def onSpawn(self):
    return
def onDeath(self):
    return
def reset(self):
    return
```

Example 4-17: The method shells for *onSpawn()*, *onDeath()*, and *reset()* that the Player, Enemy, and Asteroid classes require.

2 We will start with *Player.reset()*. The reset function will be used to ensure that an object is set to its original state and so is ready for the game to continue. It will be called both when an object respawns after death and when the game begins. Using its constructor as a starting point, consider what needs to be reset for the Player class. Position, velocity, and collision status will all need to be reset whenever a Player object spawns, so modify *Player.reset()* to match example 4-18.

```
def reset(self):
    self.rect.x = 400
    self.rect.y = 300
    self.velocityX = 0
    self.velocityY = 0
    self.collision = False
```

Example 4-18: The *Player.reset()* method returns a Player object to its starting position, ensures that it is not moving, and verifies that it is not currently colliding with anything.

```
    def onSpawn(self):
        self.reset()
    def onDeath(self):
        self.reset()
```

Example 4-19: Calling *self.reset()* from *Player.onSpawn()* and *Player.onDeath()*.

```
    def checkForCollisions(self):
        for gameObjects in self.
    collisionGroup:
        self.collision = self.rect.
    colliderect(gameObject.rect)
            if self.collision:
                    self.onDeath()
                    break
```

Example 4-20: When a Player object has a collision, call *self.onDeath()*.

③ Still working with the Player class, consider when a *Player.reset()* would need to be called. We want to reset the object when it is initially spawned and every time it is destroyed. Place a call to *self.reset()* in *Player.onSpawn()* and *Player.onDeath()*, as in example 4-19.

④ Our player ship may be built using advanced space technology, but it's still no match for an asteroid in a collision. Put a call to *self.onDeath()* in *Player.checkForCollisions()*. Now, whenever a Player object collides with anything, the Player object will be reset. This is shown in example 4-20.

⑤ Finally, put a call to *self.onSpawn()* in the Player constructor. This might seem redundant at the moment, but when we implement further game state variables we will want to know whether a Player object is being created or just being reset.

6 Now that the Player class has been set up to handle death and respawn, set up the Enemy and Asteroid classes. Beginning with Enemy, create *Enemy.reset()* to appropriately reset the object, as in example 4-21.

```
def reset(self):
    self.rect.x = 200
    self.rect.y = 200
    self.velocityX = 0
    self.velocityY = 0
```

Example 4-21: The *Enemy.reset()* method.

7 Have *Enemy.onSpawn()* and *Enemy.onDeath()* call *self.reset()*, as you did with the Player class. Example 4-22 demonstrates this. Also, call *self.onSpawn()* from the Enemy constructor.

```
onSpawn(self):
    self.reset()
onDeath(self):
    self.reset()
```

Example 4-22: Call *self.reset()* from *Enemy.onSpawn()* and *Enemy.onDeath()*.

8 For the Asteroid class, the *Asteroid.reset()* method is already set up. From *Asteroid.onSpawn()* and *Asteroid.onDeath()* call *self.reset()* and change the Asteroid constructor to call *self.onSpawn()*, instead of *self.reset()*.

9 Now that the Asteroid and Enemy classes are set up to handle *onDeath()* events, call those methods from *Player.checkForCollisions()* when *Player.collision* is true. Use a **for in** loop, as shown in example 4-25.

```
for gameObject in self.collisionGroup:
    self.collision = self.rect.
colliderect(gameObject.rect)
    if self.collision:
    self.onDeath()
    for gameObject in self.
collisionGroup:
        gameObject.onDeath()
    break
```

Example 4-23: The body of *Player.checkForCollisions()*. Call the *onDeath()* methods of all the collidable objects from *Player.checkForCollisions()* when the Player object collides with something.

Now whenever there is a collision between a Player object and any object that is in *Player.collisionGroup,* the *onDeath()* methods of every object that can trigger a collision are called. Currently, the *onDeath()* methods all reset their parent objects to their initial state.

Whenever any collision occurs in our game, the entire game is reset to its initial state and play can continue.

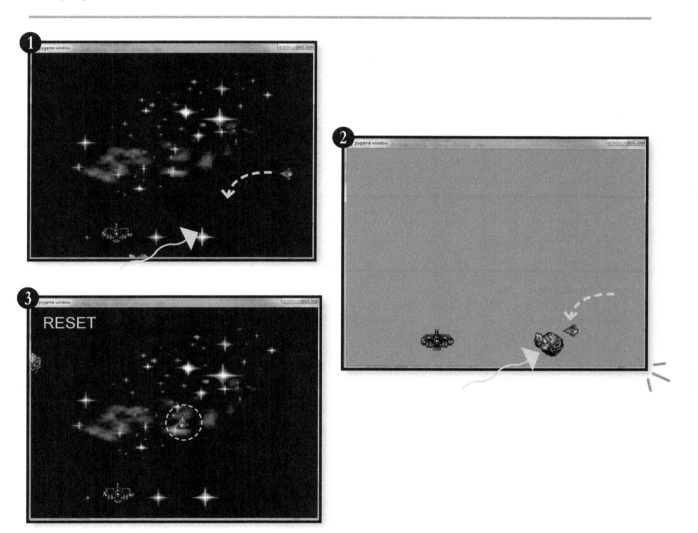

Figure 4-3: A player tries to avoid collisions, but when one happens, the game state resets and play can begin again.

The following code blocks show the *onDeath()*, *onSpawn()*, and *reset()* methods of the Asteroid, Enemy, and Player classes, and the *Player.checkForCollisions()* method.

```
def onSpawn(self):
    self.reset()
def onDeath(self):
    self.reset()
def reset(self):
    self.rect.x = random.randrange(0,self.screenX) * -1
    self.rect.y = random.randrange(0,self.screenY * -1
```

Example 4-24: The *Asteroid.onSpawn()*, *Asteroid.onDeath()* and *Asteroid.reset()* methods.

```
def onSpawn(self):
    self.reset()
def onDeath(self):
    self.reset()
def reset(self):
    self.rect.x = 200
    self.rect.y = 500
    self.velocityX = 0
    self.velocityY = 0
```

Example 4-25: The *Enemy.onSpawn()*, *Enemy.onDeath()*, and *Enemy.reset()* methods.

```
   def onSpawn(self):
      self.reset()
   def onDeath(self):
      self.reset()
   def reset(self):
      self.rect.x = 400
      self.rect.y = 300
      self.velocityX = 0
      self.velocityY = 0
      self.collision = False
```

Example 4-26: The *Player.onSpawn()*, *Player.onDeath()*, and *Player.reset()* methods.

```
   def checkForCollisions(self):
      for gameObject in self.collisionGroup:
       self.collision = self.rect.colliderect(gameObject.rect)
       if self.collision:
             self.onDeath()
             for gameObject in self.collisionGroup:
                   gameObject.onDeath()
             break
```

Example 4-27: The *Player.checkForCollisions()* method.

Now things are really starting to come together. Game objects have logic that defines their actions in the game loop and game event logic executes specific code when certain events occur during gameplay.

The transition between playing the game and starting over after a collision is very jarring, though, and that is definitely a problem. We can fix the problem with a timed delay between game events, and that is exactly what we will do in the next section.

Questions for Review:

1 What is event logic?

a Code that is executed before the main game loop.

b Code that is executed after the main game loop.

c Code that is executed when certain game events occur.

d A general term for logic that is used in game programming.

2 What is a useful starting point when creating a reset() method?

a The attributes that you think need to be reset.

b Reset everything, test the game, and remove what doesn't need to be reset.

c The values in the class constructor that may change during play.

d None of the above.

3 Using the Player.collisionGroup array lets us call the onDeath() method of every collidable object in the game.

a True.

b False.

4 Event logic allows us to ensure certain events happen in every iteration of the game loop.

a True.

b False.

4.3 Delaying Game Events

Delaying game events can make gameplay less jarring for the player. A human player who is experiencing your game needs a certain amount of time to understand what has happened and why it happened. In our simple space game, the only event that a player has to worry about at the moment is colliding with asteroids. To us, it seems blindingly obvious that the asteroid collisions are causing the game to reset, however, we have been building the game and therefore understand every aspect of the game code.

Consider someone who has never played our space game before. They might start to move the spaceship around the screen and will probably intuitively understand that they should avoid the asteroids, but when they inevitably do collide with an asteroid, the game will instantly snap them back to the starting position. There is no feedback to explain what happened or why it happened. Even a small delay between a collision and the game restarting will give the player a chance to understand the game state and make the connection between an asteroid collision and a game reset.

In this section, we will implement that exact delay as we learn how to delay game events. Delays are handled through a combination of flagging variables and timer variables.

```
import pygame, random
from imageLoader import *

playerRespawnTimer = 120 #Ticks
```

Example 4-28: The beginning of gameObjects.py, including the global variable *playerRespawnTimer*. We have noted that it is in ticks instead of milliseconds.

1 In gameObjects.py, at the top of the file outside of any Class definition, create a global variable for our timer called *playerRespawnTimer*. Set it to the value 120. This will be the amount of time we want to delay the game when we have a player respawn. We are making it globally scoped so it is consistent in Player, Asteroid, and Enemy.

Note that we have set our timer in ticks instead of milliseconds. In our game, 120 ticks is equal to 2 seconds because we are running at 60 frames per second.

2 First we will create the variables to determine if the respawn event should occur. Create the flag *self. isWaitingToRespawn* in the Player constructor and initialize it to False. Also, create a timer, *self.respawnTimer*, and set it to 0. This is shown in example 4-29.

3 When a player dies they are waiting to respawn, so in *Player.onDeath()* set *self. isWaitingToRespawn* to True and set the value of *self. respawnTimer* to the value of *playerRespawnTimer*. Finally, remove the call to *self. reset()* in *Player.onDeath()*. Example 4-30 shows how *Player.onDeath()* will look.

4 *Player.reset()* needs to be modified to reset *self. isWaitingToRespawn* to False, as in example 4-31, because on reset the player will no longer be waiting to respawn.

```
self.isWaitingToRespawn = False
self.respawnTimer = 0
self.onSpawn()
```

Example 4-29: Add *self.isWaitingToRespawn* and *self. respawnTimer* to the Player constructor and initialize them to False and 0, respectively.

```
def onDeath(self):
    self.isWaitingToRespawn = True
    self.respawnTimer =
playerRespawnTimer
```

Example 4-30: Modify *Player.onDeath()* to set *self. isWaitingToRespawn* to True and *self.respawnTimer* to the global variable *playerRespawnTimer*.

```
def reset(self):
    self.rect.x = 400
    self.rect.y = 300
    self.velocityX = 0
    self.velocityY = 0
    self.collision = False
    self.isWaitingToRespawn = False
```

Example 4-31: Modify *Player.reset()* to reset the value of *self. isWaitingToRespawn*.

```
def update(self):
    #Check if object is waiting to
respawn
    if self.isWaitingToRespawn:
      self.respawnTimer -= 1
      if self.respawnTimer <= 0:
            self.reset()
    else:
      #Process player input
      controls = self.getPlayerInput()
      self.processControl(controls)
      self.image = pygame.transform.
rotate(self.asset, self.angle)

      #Collision Detection
      self.checkForCollisions()

      #Update physics
      self.updatePhysics()
```

Example 4-32: *Player.update() after implementing the delay logic.*

Our flags and timing variables are set, so we will use them in *Player. update()* to freeze the player and delay the execution of *Player. reset()* for two seconds.

5 In *Player.update()*, build an **if else** statement that checks to see if *self. isWaitingToRespawn* is true. If it is, first decrement the value of *self.respawnTimer* and then check if the value of *self.respawnTimer* is 0 or less. If it is, then the game has iterated through 120 game loops, so execute *self.reset()*.

6 In the **else** block run the existing *Player. update()* code. Example 4-32 shows *Player.update()*.

The code that we have just created uses a set number of iterations through the game loop to create a delay. We have used **Pygame.time.Clock.tick()** to limit our game to 60 frames per second, so we know that 120 iterations through our game loop will equate to 2 seconds. There are other methods of implementing delays in Pygame and in other game engines.

Now when you run the game you will see that after a collision the player ship freezes in place for two seconds before respawning, but the asteroids continue to move. This is happening because we implemented the delay for the Player class but not for the Asteroid or Enemy classes. The techniques that we will use to implement delays for the Asteroid and Enemy classes are exactly the same as what we have done for the Player class.

7 Implement the *self. isWaitingToRespawn* flag and *self.respawnTimer* variable in the Enemy and Asteroid class constructors, as in example 4-33.

```
self.isWaitingToRespawn = False
self.respawnTimer = 0
self.onSpawn()
```

Example 4-33: Implement the flag and timer variable in the Enemy and Asteroid constructors.

8 In the *Enemy.onDeath()* and *Asteroid.onDeath()* methods, remove the calls to *self.reset()* and replace them by setting the *self.isWaitingToRespawn* flags to True and the *self. respawnTimer* variables to the value of *playerRespawnTimer*, shown in example 4-34.

```
def onDeath(self):
    self.isWaitingToRespawn = True
    self.respawnTimer =
playerRespawnTimer
```

Example 4-34: Modify the *onDeath()* methods of the Enemy and Asteroid classes.

9 In the *Enemy.reset()* and *Asteroid.reset()* methods, reset the values of the *self. isWaitingToRespawn* flags to False. *Enemy.reset()* is shown in example 4-35 and *Asteroid. reset()* is shown in example 4-36.

```
def reset(self):
    self.rect.x = 200
    self.rect.y = 500
    self.velocityX = 0
    self.velocityY = 0
    self.isWaitingToRespawn = false
```

Example 4-35: Modify the *Enemy.reset()* method.

10 Finally, in the *Enemy. update()* and *Asteroid.update()* methods create a **for in** loop that matches *Player.update()* and delays the execution of *self.reset()* until *self. respawnTimer* is less than 0 if *self.isWaitingToRespawn* is true. Examples 4-37 and 4-38 on the next page demonstrate this.

```
def reset(self):
    self.rect.x = random.randrange(0,-
self.screenX) * -1
    self.rect.y = random.randrange(0,-
self.screenY) * -1
    self.isWaitingToRespawn = False
```

Example 4-36: Modify the *Asteroid.reset()* method.

```
def update(self):
    #Check if object is waiting to respawn
    if self.isWaitingToRespawn:
     self.respawnTimer -= 1
     if self.respawnTimer <= 0:
            self.reset()
    else:
     self.velocityX += self.accelerationX
     self.velocityY += self.accelerationY
     self.rect.x += self.velocityX
     self.rect.y += self.velocityY
```

Example 4-37: The *Enemy.update()* method.

```
def update(self):
    #Check if object is waiting to respawn
    if self.isWaitingToRespawn:
     self.respawnTimer -= 1
     if self.respawnTimer <= 0:
            self.reset()
    else:
     self.velocityX += self.accelerationX
     self.velocityY += self.accelerationY
     self.rect.x += self.velocityX
     self.rect.y += self.velocityY
     if self.rect.x >= self.rect.width + self.screenX or self.rect.y >= self.
   rect.height + self.screenY:
            self.reset()
```

Example 4-38: The *Asteroid.update()* method.

Now when you run the game, every game object pauses for two seconds after a collision. This gives the player time to understand what happened and to prepare for the game to begin again.

```
# Game Loop Template
import pygame, sys
from gameObjects import *

pygame.init()
#Create the application window
screenXY = (800,600)
screen = pygame.display.set_mode(screenXY)

#Create the game objects
background = Background(
                "images/Nebula1.bmp", screen.get_width(),
            screen.get_height()
            )
player = Player("images/Hunter1.bmp", 2, (25,1,23,23), (0,0,0) )

gameObjects = []
gameObjects.append(player)
for i in range(3):
    enemy = Enemy("images/SpaceStation.bmp", 1, (101,13,91,59), (69,78,91) )
    gameObjects.append(enemy)
    player.collisionGroup.append(enemy)
for i in range(5):
    asteroid = Asteroid(
                "images/Rock2a.bmp", 1, (6,3,80,67), (69,78,91),
                screenXY
                )
    gameObjects.append(asteroid)
    player.collisionGroup.append(asteroid)

#Create the game clock
clock = pygame.time.Clock()
```

```
#The game loop
while True:
    for event in pygame.event.get():
    if event.type == pygame.QUIT:
            pygame.quit()

    #Update the game state
    for gameObject in gameObjects:
     gameObject.update()

    #Display the game updates
    if player.collision:
     screen.fill( (255,0,0) )
    else:
     screen.blit(background.image, (background.rect.x, background.rect.y) )
    for gameObject in gameObjects:
     screen.blit(gameObject.image, (gameObject.rect.x, gameObject.rect.y) )

    pygame.display.flip()
    clock.tick(60)
```

Example 4-39: The complete for main.py.

```
import pygame, random
from imageLoader import *

playerRespawnTimer = 120 #Ticks

class Background(pygame.sprite.Sprite):
    def __init__(self, image, width, height):
      self.originalAsset = pygame.image.load(image)
      self.image = pygame.transform.scale(self.originalAsset, (width,height))
      self.rect = self.image.get_rect()
    def update(self):
      return

class Player(pygame.sprite.Sprite):
    def __init__(self, image, scale, clip, ckey):
      self.asset = imageLoader(image, scale, clip)
      self.image = self.asset
      self.image.set_colorkey(ckey)
      self.rect = self.image.get_rect()
      self.rect.x = 400
      self.rect.y = 300
      self.velocityX = 0
      self.velocityY = 0
      self.maxVelocity = 8
      self.accelerationX = 0
      self.accelerationY = 0
      self.thrust = .5
      self.damping = 0.3
      self.angle = 0
      self.collision = False
      self.collisionGroup = []
      self.isWaitingToRespawn = False
      self.respawnTimer = 0
      self.onSpawn()

    def onSpawn(self):
      self.reset()
```

```
def onDeath(self):
 self.isWaitingToRespawn = True
 self.respawnTimer = playerRespawnTimer

def reset(self):
 self.rect.x = 400
 self.rect.y = 300
 self.velocityX = 0
 self.velocityY = 0
 self.collision = False
 self.isWaitingToRespawn = False

def update(self):
 #Check if object is waiting to respawn
 if self.isWaitingToRespawn:
        self.respawnTimer -= 1
        if self.respawnTimer <= 0:
                self.reset()
 else:
 #Process player input
 controls = self.getPlayerInput()
 self.processControl(controls)
 self.image = pygame.transform.rotate(self.asset, self.angle)

 #Collision Detection
 self.checkForCollisions()

 #Update physics
 self.updatePhysics()

def checkForCollisions(self):
 for gameObject in self.collisionGroup:
        self.collision = self.rect.colliderect(gameObject.rect)
        if self.collision:
                self.onDeath()
                for gameObject in self.collisionGroup:
                        gameObject.onDeath()
                break
```

```
def updatePhysics(self):
 self.velocityX += self.accelerationX
 self.velocityY += self.accelerationY

 #Apply damping horizontal
 if self.velocityX < 0 - self.damping:
      self.velocityX += self.damping
 elif self.velocityX > 0 + self.damping:
      self.velocityX -= self.damping
 else:
      self.velocityX = 0
 #Apply damping vertical
 if self.velocityY < 0 - self.damping:
      self.velocityY += self.damping
 elif self.velocityY > 0 + self.damping:
      self.velocityY -= self.damping
 else:
      self.velocityY = 0

 #Cap max velocity
 if self.velocityX > self.maxVelocity:
      self.velocityX = self.maxVelocity
 if self.velocityX < self.maxVelocity * -1:
      self.velocityX = self.maxVelocity * -1
 if self.velocityY > self.maxVelocity:
      self.velocityY = self.maxVelocity
 if self.velocityY < self.maxVelocity * -1:
      self.velocityY = self.maxVelocity * -1

 self.rect.x += self.velocityX
 self.rect.y += self.velocityY

def getPlayerInput(self):
 up = pygame.key.get_pressed()[pygame.K_UP]
 right = pygame.key.get_pressed()[pygame.K_RIGHT]
 down = pygame.key.get_pressed()[pygame.K_DOWN]
 left = pygame.key.get_pressed()[pygame.K_LEFT]
 return up,right,down,left
```

```
def processControl(self, control):
    if control[0] and control[3]:
        self.angle = 45
    elif control[0] and control[1]:
        self.angle = 315
    elif control[1] and control[2]:
        self.angle = 225
    elif control[2] and control[3]:
        self.angle = 135
    elif control[0]:
        self.angle = 0
    elif control[1]:
        self.angle = 270
    elif control[2]:
        self.angle = 180
    elif control[3]:
        self.angle = 90
    self.accelerationX = self.thrust * (control[1] - control[3])
    self.accelerationY = self.thrust * (control[2] - control[0])

class Enemy(pygame.sprite.Sprite):
    def __init__(self, image, scale, clip, ckey):
        self.image = imageLoader(image, scale, clip)
        self.image.set_colorkey(ckey)
        self.rect = self.image.get_rect()
        self.rect.x = 200
        self.rect.y = 500
        self.velocityX = 0
        self.velocityY = 0
        self.accelerationX = 0
        self.accelerationY = 0
        self.isWaitingToRespawn = False
        self.respawnTimer = 0
        self.onSpawn()
```

```
def update(self):
 #Check if object is waiting to respawn
 if self.isWaitingToRespawn:
        self.respawnTimer -= 1
        if self.respawnTimer <= 0:
               self.reset()
 else:
        self.velocityX += self.accelerationX
        self.velocityY += self.accelerationY
        self.rect.x += self.velocityX
        self.rect.y += self.velocityY
def onSpawn(self):
 self.reset()
def onDeath(self):
 self.isWaitingToRespawn = True
 self.respawnTimer = playerRespawnTimer
def reset(self):
 self.rect.x = 200
 self.rect.y = 500
 self.velocityX = 0
 self.velocityY = 0
 self.isWaitingToRespawn = False

class Asteroid(pygame.sprite.Sprite):
   def __init__(self, image, scale, clip, ckey, screenXY):
    self.image = imageLoader(image, scale, clip)
    self.image.set_colorkey(ckey)
    self.rect = self.image.get_rect()
    self.velocityX = 6
    self.velocityY = 6
    self.accelerationX = 0
    self.accelerationY = 0
    self.screenX = screenXY[0]
    self.screenY = screenXY[1]
    self.isWaitingToRespawn = False
    self.respawnTimer = 0
    self.onSpawn()
```

```
    def update(self):
    #Check if object is waiting to respawn
    if self.isWaitingToRespawn:
            self.respawnTimer -= 1
            if self.respawnTimer <= 0:
                    self.reset()
    else:
            self.velocityX += self.accelerationX
            self.velocityY += self.accelerationY
            self.rect.x += self.velocityX
            self.rect.y += self.velocityY
            if self.rect.x >= self.rect.width + self.screenX or self.rect.y >=
    self.rect.height + self.screenY:
                    self.reset()
    def onSpawn(self):
    self.reset()
    def onDeath(self):
    self.isWaitingToRespawn = True
    self.respawnTimer = playerRespawnTimer
    def reset(self):
    self.rect.x = random.randrange(0,self.screenX) * -1
    self.rect.y = random.randrange(0,self.screenY) * -1
    self.isWaitingToRespawn = False
```

Example 4-40: The complete gameObjects.py file.

Your game is really starting to take shape! Now players can move their ship around the screen, dodge clear obstacles that come in endless waves, and when the player is struck by an obstacle, the game resets. Things are starting to come together.

In this chapter we have learned how to use game logic that is attached to objects to execute code during the game loop. We have also learned how to use logic that is tied to events to execute code when only certain conditions are met. We then used delays to time the execution of events in order to create clearer, more rewarding gameplay.

In the next chapter, we will add logic to our enemies through simple enemy artificial intelligence. We will also create logic to manage the player's progression through the game to make the player's experience more interesting.

Questions for Review:

1 What is a good reason to delay game events?

    a To make the game less jarring for a player.

    b To give the player an opportunity to get refreshments.

    c To ensure that the game loop is able to complete processing.

    d Game events should never be delayed.

2 In a game running at 60 frames per second, how many seconds is 180 ticks?

    a 2.

    b 5.

    c 1.

    d 3.

3 In our game, we only need to implement a delay for the Player class.

    a True.

    b False.

4 What do we use to create delays?

    a Flagging variables and timer variables.

    b Timer variables only.

    c Flagging variables and the system clock.

    d A "pause" key and the player's wristwatch.

CHAPTER 04 LAB EXERCISE

In this lab exercise, you will use the console to simulate power ups. This will expose you to only the core logic for enabling power ups in a game.

1 Create an invincibility power up:

a) Once collected, the player will be invincible for a set amount of time.

b) If a second invincibility power up is collected while one is in use, the timer will be reset.

2 Create a bomb power up:

a) The player can collect an unlimited number of bombs.

3 Simulate collecting and using power ups:

a) Simulate collecting an invincibility power up by pressing the "1" key.

b) Simulate collecting a bomb power up by pressing the "2" key.

c) Simulate firing a bomb power up by pressing the space bar.

```
>>>
Collected Invincibility
Invincibility Started
Collected Invincibility
Invincibility Started
Invincibility Ended
Collected a Bomb
Collected a Bomb
Collected a Bomb
Used Bomb
Used Bomb
Used Bomb
No Bombs to Use
```

The expected console output of this lab exercise.

Adding
Enemies

Chapter Objectives:

- You will learn how to create simple enemy AI.
- You will understand more complex forms of AI.
- You will create a simple state machine.
- You will learn how to track progression in a game.

5.1 Simple Enemy AI

Our space game has asteroid obstacles that move across the screen, and a player ship that is controlled by a simple physics engine. We also spawn enemies, but so far we have not been using them. Creating enemies requires more complicated logic than creating asteroids because enemies will be active agents in the game world for the player to interact with, instead of passive obstacles that the player must avoid. In order to implement enemies, we need to create some rudimentary artificial intelligence, or AI, to control their behavior.

In video games, artificial intelligence is the intelligent behavior of non-playable characters. The asteroids are simple objects that follow one simple action regardless of the player's actions, but we need the enemies to react to the player in an intelligent way. Of course, in this situation "intelligence" is relative — we are only going to be creating simple AI routines for our enemies. Later in the chapter we will introduce the idea of state machines to create more complicated behaviors, but first we will just create enemies that chase the player around the screen. Load gameObjects.py and main.py.

> **Artificial intelligence**
>
> In video games, the intelligent behavior of non-playable characters.

1 First, we need to get our Enemy objects off of the screen. We will have them spawn in the same region of space as the Asteroid objects. We can use the spawning logic from *Asteroid.reset()* to implement this in *Enemy.reset()*, as shown in example 1-1.

```
def reset(self):
    self.rect.x = random.randrange(0,
self.screenX) * -1
    self.rect.y = random.randrange(0,
self.screenY) * -1
    self.velocityX = 0
    self.velocityY = 0
    self.isWaitingToRespawn = False
```

Example 5-1: Updating *Enemy.reset()* to spawn enemies off of the main screen.

Now when you run the game there will only be a lonely player ship awaiting some incoming asteroids. The Enemy objects will stay where they spawn because they have no logic telling them to move. We could just assign some values to their *Enemy. velocityX* and *Enemy.velocityY* attributes to get them moving, but we want them to move according to the location of the player. Our goal is for our enemy ships to follow the player around the screen.

In order to do this, we will use vectors. A vector is a way to describe the movement from one point in space to another. The distance and direction from the Enemy object to the Player object is a vector. In any given frame of our game loop, both the Enemy and Player objects will have set coordinates. To get from the Enemy object to the Player object, there has to be some amount of movement along the X axis and then some amount of movement on the Y axis. There is also a direct line from the Enemy object to the Player object. Taken as a whole, we have a right triangle with the hypotenuse representing the distance and direction between the Enemy object and the Player object. That hypotenuse is the vector that we are concerned with, and its length is our vector length.

We do not want the Enemy object to move all the way to the Player object in a single frame, though. Instead, we only want the Enemy object to go a certain part of the distance to the Player. How far the Enemy moves will be dependent on the object's velocity attributes, so we need to normalize our vector in order to use it to determine those velocities. A normalized vector is a vector whose length is 1.

This is a complicated idea, but a simple way to visualize it is to picture a right triangle with the player and the enemy as the endpoints of its hypotenuse. Now, imagine the hypotenuse getting smaller and smaller until it's only as long as the distance that you want the enemy to move in a single frame. Finally, picture a new right triangle based off of that hypotenuse. The legs of the triangle are how far the enemy has to move along the X and Y axes in a single frame.

The distance that you want the enemy to move per frame may change, but no matter what it is, it can always be considered one unit of enemy movement. This is where the normalization comes in — for each frame, you will calculate the vector between the Enemy object and Player object and then normalize the vector so that it represents one unit of Enemy movement. Then you calculate how far along the X and Y axes the Enemy has to travel to reach one unit of Enemy movement, based on the object's speed attributes.

1 Calculate the whole original **vector.**

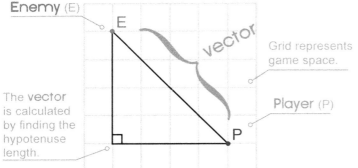

Enemy (E)

Grid represents game space.

The **vector** is calculated by finding the hypotenuse length.

Player (P)

2 The **vector** is normalized based on the enemy's max velocity.

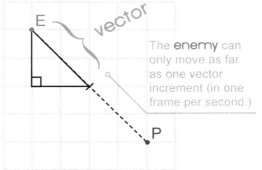

The **enemy** can only move as far as one vector increment (in one frame per second.)

3 The **enemy** moves towards the player along the target vector.

The **enemy's** X and Y coordinates are modified by the values of the legs of the triangle.

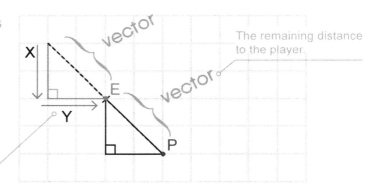

The remaining distance to the player.

4 In the next frame, when the **player** moves a new **vector** is calculated and the enemy's direction changes accordingly.

A new **vector** is calculated for the new player location.

Player moves...

The **vector** unit adjusts to point to the player's new position.

Figure 5-1: Determining the target vector for an Enemy object.

```
for i in range(3):
    enemy = Enemy("images/SpacStor.bmp",
1, (101,13,91,59), (69,78,91), screenXY,
player)
    gameObjects.append(enemy)
    player.collisionGroup.append(enemy)
```

Example 5-2: Passing *player* as an argument to the Enemy class constructor.

```
def __init__(self, image, sclae, clip,
ckey, screenXY, gameObjectTarget)
    self.target = gameObjectTarget
```

Example 5-3: Create a parameter in the Enemy class constructor for an Enemy object's target.

```
targetVectorX = self.target.rect.x -
self.rect.x
targetVectorY = self.target.rect.y -
self.rect.y
distance = math.sqrt((targetVectorX)**2
+ (targetVectorY)**2)
```

Example 5-4: In *Enemy.update()*, determine the vector from the Enemy object to its target.

```
import pygame, random, math
```

Example 5-5: Ensure that the math library is imported so that math.sqrt() can be used.

2 Enemy objects need to have a target. In main.py, pass *player* as an argument when creating the Enemy objects, as shown in example 5-2.

3 In the Enemy class in gameObjects.py, add a *gameObjectTarget* parameter to the constructor and create a *self.target* attribute that is set to *gameObjectTarget*. This is shown in example 5-3.

4 In *Enemy.update()*, if the enemy is not waiting to respawn, create two variables, *targetVectorX* and *targetVectorY*, and set them to the difference between the Enemy object's position and the target position, as shown in example 5-4.

5 After getting the *targetVectorX* and *targetVectorY* values calculate the distance from the Enemy object to the target using the pythagorean theorem, as shown in example 5-4. Also, import math in gameObjects.py to use **math.sqrt()**, as in example 5-5.

```
targetVectorX = targetVectorX / distance
targetVectorY = targetVectorY / distance
```

Example 5-6: Normalize the vector so that the values are based on scale of 1.

6 Now that we have the vector from the Enemy object to its target, we need to normalize the vector, as shown in example 5-6.

7 We can test our enemy movement with the normalized vector. First, to make things simpler, modify main.py so that the Asteroid objects are not added to *player.collisionGroup*, as shown in example 5-7.

```
for i in range(5):
    asteroid = Asteroid("images/
Rock2a.bmp", 1, (6,3,80,67), (69,78,91),
screenXY)
    gameObjects.append(asteroid)
    #player.collisionGroup.append
(asteroid)
```

Example 5-7: Make Asteroid objects non-collidable to simplify Enemy object testing.

8 Back in gameObjects.py, modify *Enemy.update()* so that *self.velocityX* and *self.velocityY* uses the normalized vectors. Set speed values to move the Enemy objects towards the player, as shown in example 5-8.

9 Test the game out! The enemies should move from off screen and follow the player's ship around.

```
targetVectorX = self.target.rect.x -
self.rect.x
targetVectorY = self.target.rect.y -
self.rect.y
distance = math.sqrt((targetVectorX)**2
+ (targetVectorY)**2)

targetVectorX = targetVectorX / distance
targetVectorY = targetVectorY / distance

#Start physics
self.velocityX = targetVectorX * 5
self.velocityY = targetVectorY * 5
self.rect.x += self.velocityX
self.rect.y += self.velocityY
```

Example 5-8: The normalized vectors will make Enemy objects constantly move towards their target.

Now we have enemies that chase the player around. Great!

The Enemy objects' movement is visibly different from the player's, and that's something that we should fix. We have a complete physics system for our Player class and we can quickly implement that in the Enemy class.

The main difference between our Player class physics and our Enemy class physics is that we are replacing acceleration based on player input with acceleration based on target vectors.

```
▶   self.accelerationX = 0
▶   self.accelerationY = 0
▶   self.velocityX = 0
▶   self.velocityY = 0
▶   self.thrust = 0.5
▶   self.damping = 0.3
▶   self.maxVelocity = 6
```

Example 5-9: Initialize the physics attributes of the Enemy class in its constructor.

```
▶   #Start physics
▶   self.accelerationX = targetVectorX *
    self.thrust
▶   self.accelerationY = targetVectorY *
    self.thrust
▶   self.velocityX += self.accelerationX
▶   self.velocityY += self.accelerationY
```

Example 5-10: Use the target vectors to determine the Enemy object's acceleration.

10 In the Enemy class constructor, initialize the physics attributes *self.accelerationX*, *self.accelerationY*, *self.velocityX*, *self.velocityY*, *self.thrust*, *self.damping*, and *self.maxVelocity*. Keep the value of *self.maxVelocity* lower than the value of *Player.maxVelocity* so that the player has a chance to escape. This is shown in example 5-9.

11 Modify *Enemy.update()* to calculate *self.accelerationX* and *self.accelerationY* using the *self.thrust* value and the target vectors.

12 Modify *self.velocityX* and *self.velocityY* by *self.accelerationX* and *self.accelerationY* as we did in the Player class. These steps are shown in example 5-10.

13 Now we need to implement damping and limit our maximum velocity, as we have done in the Player class. The code will be identical. Once that is complete, update the position of the Enemy object by modifying *self.rect.x* and *self.rect.y*. Example 5-11 demonstrates this code.

```
#Start physics
self.accelerationX = targetVectorX *
self.thrust
self.accelerationY = targetVectorY *
self.thrust
self.velocityX += self.accelerationX
self.velocityY += self.accelerationY

#Apply damping horizontal
if self.velocityX < 0 - self.damping:
    self.velocityX += self.damping
elif self.velocityX > 0 + self.damping:
    self.velocityX -= self.damping
else self.velocityX = 0
#Apply damping vertical
if self.velocityY < 0 - self.damping:
    self.velocityY += self.damping
elif self.velocityY > 0 + self.damping:
    self.velocityY -= self.damping
else self.velocityY = 0

#Cap max velocity
if self.velocityX > self.maxVelocity:
    self.velocityX = self.maxVelocity
if self.velocityX < self.maxVelocity*-1:
    self.velocityX = self.maxVelocity*-1
if self.velocityY > self.maxVelocity:
    self.velocityY = self.maxVelocity
if self.velocityY < self.maxVelocity*-1:
    self.velocityY = self.maxVelocity*-1

#Change position:
self.rect.x += self.velocityX
self.rect.y += self.velocityY
```

Example 5-11: Applying the Player class physics to the Enemy class.

Now Enemy objects follow the same movement rules as the player, but at a slightly lower speed to give the player a chance to evade them. Awesome! You can take some time to fine tune the attributes that govern Enemy object movement so that the game feels the way you like. Below is the complete code from the *Enemy.update()* method that we worked on in this section.

```python
def update(self):
    #Check if object is waiting to respawn
    if self.isWaitingToRespawn:
        self.respawnTimer -= 1
        if self.respawnTimer <= 0:
            self.reset()
    else:
        targetVectorX = self.target.rect.x - self.rect.x
        targetVectorY = self.target.rect.y - self.rect.y
        distance = math.sqrt((targetVectorX)**2 + (targetVectorY)**2)
        targetVectorX = targetVectorX / distance
        targetVectorY = targetVectorY / distance

        #Start physics
        self.accelerationX = targetVectorX * self.thrust
        self.accelerationY = targetVectorY * self.thrust
        self.velocityX += self.accelerationX
        self.velocityY += self.accelerationY
        #Apply damping horizontal
        if self.velocityX < 0 - self.damping:
            self.velocityX += self.damping
        elif self.velocityX > 0 + self.damping:
            self.velocityX -= self.damping
        else self.velocityX = 0
        #Apply damping vertical
        if self.velocityY < 0 - self.damping:
            self.velocityY += self.damping
        elif self.velocityY > 0 + self.damping:
            self.velocityY -= self.damping
        else self.velocityY = 0
```

```
#Cap max velocity
if self.velocityX > self.maxVelocity:
    self.velocityX = self.maxVelocity
if self.velocityX < self.maxVelocity * -1:
    self.velocityX = self.maxVelocity * -1
if self.velocityY > self.maxVelocity:
    self.velocityY = self.maxVelocity
if self.velocityY < self.maxVelocity * -1:
    self.velocityY = self.maxVelocity * -1

#Change position:
self.rect.x += self.velocityX
self.rect.y += self.velocityY
```

Example 5-12: The complete *Enemy.update()* method from gameObjects.py.

In this section we have included some simple AI that instructs the Enemy objects to constantly follow the player. In the next section, we will create more advanced logic and introduce a simple state machine.

Questions for Review:

1 What is artificial intelligence in video games?

    a A method of determining the skill level of the player.

    b The intelligent behavior of non-playable characters.

    c A means of controlling non-interactive objects.

    d Artificial intelligence is not used in video games.

2 What is a vector?

    a A Pygame variable type.

    b The result of a function that moves an object.

    c A Pygame built-in enemy type.

    d A way to describe movement from one point in space to another.

3 In order to use vectors in our AI programming, we need to normalize them.

    a True.

    b False.

4 What do we use as the basis for acceleration in the Enemy class physics?

    a Target vectors.

    b Player input.

    c Random numbers.

    d Enemy orientation.

5.2 More Enemy AI

Currently, the enemy ships will find and track the player relentlessly. While it's easy to admire their tenacity, this doesn't make for a very interesting game. In this section, we will add more advanced AI to change the behavior of the enemy ships by having them give chase when the player's ship is within a certain range, while allowing them to travel in a set direction when the player is not in range.

We could do this using a simple conditional to check the distance between an Enemy object and its target, however, we will instead create a simple state machine. A state machine is an abstract machine that can be in one of a set number of states. The state that a state machine is in at a given time is known as its current state, and a change to another state, known as a state transition, occurs when there is a triggering event or condition.

For our purposes, the state machine will determine the Enemy object's behavior. We will have three states — searching, chasing, and lost chase — that we will transition between.

State Machine

An abstract machine that can be in one of a set number of states and can transition to different states according to triggering events or conditions.

① First we will set up our state machine. In the Enemy class, create *Enemy. processStates()* and build the **if elif** shell seen in example 5-13.

② Add *self.state* to *Enemy. reset()* and set it to 1 so that Enemy objects are looking for the player by default.

```
def processStates(self):
    #Get target vectors
    #Enemy is searching for player
    if self.state = 1:

    #Enemy is chasing player
    elif self.state = 2:

    #Enemy lost chase
    elif self.state = 3:
```

Example 5-13: The state machine shell in *Enemy. processStates()*

```
  def processStates(self):
    #Get target vectors
    targetVectorX = self.target.rect.x -
self.rect.x
    targetVectorY = self.target.rect.y -
self.rect.y
    distance = math.sqrt
((targetVectorX)**2 +
(targetVectorY)**2)
```

Example 5-14: The states depend on the target's location.

```
  #Enemy is searching for player
  if self.state == 1:
    if distance <= self.detectionRange:
      self.state = 2
    else:
      self.accelerationX = self.thrust
      self.accelerationY = self.thrust


  #Enemy is chasing playe
  elif self.state == 2:
    if distance > self.detectionRange:
      self.state = 3
    else:
      targetVectorX = targetVectorX /
distance
      targetVectorY = targetVectorY /
distance
      self.accelerationX = targetVectorX *
self.thrust
      self.accelerationY = targetVectorY *
self.thrust

  #Enemy lost chase
  elif self.state == 3:
    self.accelerationX = self.thrust
    self.accelerationY = self.thrust
```

Example 5-15: The three states for an Enemy object.

3 In the Enemy constructor, create *self.detectionRange* and set it to 300. This will be the distance at which Enemy objects can detect the player.

4 The transitions between states are determined by the distance that the Enemy object is from its target, so *Enemy.processStates()* needs the target vector information. Remove it from *Enemy.update()* and implement it in *Enemy.processStates()*, as shown in example 5-14.

5 The initial state will trigger a transition if a target is within *self.detectionRange*. If not, the Enemy object will continue on its course.

6 The second state will trigger a transition when a target goes outside of *self.detectionRange*. If not, the Enemy object will chase its target.

7 The final state has no transition and will set the Enemy object back on its original course. Example 5-15 shows the state machine code.

The *Enemy.processStates()* method handles the target vectors and sets the values of *self.accelerationX* and *self.accelerationY* so *Enemy.update()* will need to be modified. *Enemy.update()* should call *self.processStates()* first to ensure that *self.accelerationX* and *self.accelerationY* are set, and then handle the remaining physics calculations.

As the program is currently written, after an Enemy object enters state 3 it will continue off into oblivion. We do not want this — instead, we want the enemy to respawn in the same manner that Asteroid objects respawn.

---

8 In *Enemy.update()* remove the code that sets *self.accelerationX* and *self.accelerationY* and replace it with a call to *self.processStates()*, as in example 5-16. Acceleration is handled according to the state that an Enemy object is in.

```
#Check states
self.processStates()
#Start physics
self.velocityX += self.accelerationX
self.velocityY += self.accelerationY
```

Example 5-16: Acceleration is set within *Enemy.processStates()*.

9 In *Enemy.update()*, after the physics calculations are complete, test the location of the Enemy object. As with the Asteroid object, if the Enemy object is no longer visible, respawn it. The code is shown in example 5-17. Note that we have called *self.onDeath()* instead of *self.reset()*. We did this because the delay implemented in *self.onDeath()* gives the player a moment's respite between escaping one enemy and having the next enemy spawn.

```
#Check bounds
if self.rect.x >= self.rect.width +
self.screenX or self.rect.y >= self.
rect.height + self.screenY:
    self.onDeath()
```

Example 5-17: If the Enemy object is no longer visible, respawn it off screen.

Now when you run your game there will be enemies that spawn in a searching state and move in a set direction. Once they detect the player's ship, they will enter a chase state and pursue the player until the player is able to get out of range. Once that happens, the enemies will enter a third state, lost chase, and continue on their original trajectory until they are no longer visible. At that point, they will respawn in their initial state after a two second delay. If any of the enemies are able to catch the player, the game will stop, and after two seconds every game object will be reset.

Congratulations, your game is really starting to come along! In this section we have introduced only a very simple state machine, however the concept of the state machine is at the core of computer science. In fact, state machines are everywhere in modern life - vending machines, traffic lights, or turnstiles are all examples of state machines.

State 1: *The enemies move in a set direction (down and right.)*

State 3: *The enemies have lost track of the player and are continuing in the original direction.*

State 2: *The enemies actively change course and follow the player.*

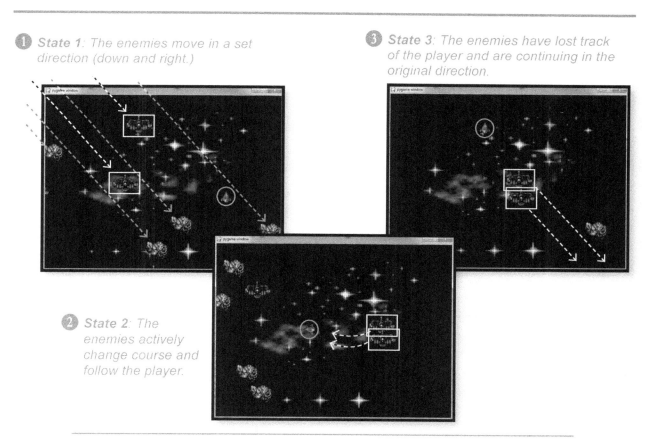

Figure 5-2: The Enemy objects behave differently depending on the state that they are in.

```
def processStates(self):
    #Get target vectors
    targetVectorX = self.target.rect.x - self.rect.x
    targetVectorY = self.target.rect.y - self.rect.y
    distance = math.sqrt((targetVectorX)**2 + (targetVectorY)**2)
    #Enemy is searching for player
    if self.state == 1:
     if distance <= self.detectionRange:
            self.state = 2
     else:
            self.accelerationX = self.thrust
            self.accelerationY = self.thrust

    #Enemy is chasing playe
    elif self.state == 2:
     if distance > self.detectionRange:
            self.state = 3
     else:
            targetVectorX = targetVectorX / distance
            targetVectorY = targetVectorY / distance
            self.accelerationX = targetVectorX * self.thrust
            self.accelerationY = targetVectorY * self.thrust

    #Enemy lost chase
    elif self.state == 3:
     self.accelerationX = self.thrust
     self.accelerationY = self.thrust
```

Example 5-18: The complete *Enemy.processStates()*.

Questions for Review:

1 What is a state machine?

a An abstract machine that can be in one of a set number of states.

b An abstract machine that only exists in a single, predetermined state.

c A Pygame built-in class.

d A Python method to handle object states.

2 What is the term for a change between one state and another state in a state machine?

a Change.

b Modification.

c Transition.

d Differentiation.

3 How many states can a state machine have?

a Three.

b Seven.

c Eleventeen.

d There is no hard limit.

4 Is a vending machine an example of a state machine?

a Yes.

b No.

5.3 Game Progression Logic

With all of the game objects designed and functioning properly and the AI implemented, the gameplay in our space game is complete. There are obstacles to be avoided and enemies to engage with. The game itself is far from complete, though. In this section, we will look into implementing logic to control game progression.

Controlling and managing the overall game state is very important because it allows you to create progression and give your players a sense of accomplishment. In many modern games, progression is implemented through movement to new levels or environments, and is often connected to a story. Progression also connects deeply with gameplay because games tend to get harder as they go. Ideally, a game will progress from introducing the player to gameplay concepts through to mastery of those concepts before introducing new ones. Ultimately, all of the skills the player learned become viable and allow mastery of the game. This progress loop keeps a game feeling fresh, interesting, and exciting.

Our space game only has a few simple gameplay elements, so progression is going to be similarly simple, however, the basic elements will demonstrate how game state management works and how game progression logic can be implemented.

Our space game currently spawns three enemies and they attack the player in a wave. We are going to introduce progression by increasing the number of enemies per wave up to a set maximum. In order to do this, we will need to create a class, WaveManager, to control when Enemy objects will attack. To do this, the WaveManager class will need to keep track of the number of Enemy objects currently attacking the player, the maximum number of Enemy objects that are allowed to attack the player, and how many waves have attacked the player.

Open up main.py and gameObjects.py. First, in gameObjects.py, we will create the WaveManager class.

```
class WaveManager():
    def __init__(self, initWaveSize,
maxWaveSize):
        self.currentWave = 0
        self.activeNumber = 0
        self.maxWaveSize = maxWaveSize
        self.initWaveSize = initWaveSize
        self.waveSize = self.initWaveSize
        self.enemyList = []
```

Example 5-19: The attributes that the WaveManager class will need.

1 At the end of gameObjects.py, create a new class named WaveManager.

2 In the WaveManager's constructor, consider what we will need to keep track of. We want to know the current wave, the number of active enemies, the maximum wave size, the initial wave size, the current wave size, and we will want to store a list of the Enemy objects to be managed.

3 Also, think about what arguments we would want to pass to the constructor. We want to be able to set the initial size of waves and the maximum allowable size of waves.

4 The current wave will be initialized at 0 because the game will start before the first wave is launched, and the number of active enemies will also start at 0. Example 5-19 displays the WaveManager class definition and its class constructor.

Now that we have an idea of what attributes our WaveManager class needs, we have to consider what we want it to do.

First and foremost, we want our WaveManager class to manage Enemy object spawning. Recall that we are not creating and destroying objects - rather, we are reusing objects. What we really need to do with our Enemy objects is determine if they are going to be active or inactive.

We need to know what to do when either an Enemy object or the player dies, and we need to know how to set up a new, progressively more challenging, gameplay wave.

Finally, we need to know whether or not it's time to launch a wave.

5 Create the outlines of the required methods. We will have *WaveManager. activateEnemies()*, *WaveManager.enemyDie()*, *WaveManager.playerDie()*, *WaveManager.nextWave()*, and *WaveManager.update()*. Example 5-20 shows this code.

```
def activateEnemies(self):
    #Set enemies to active
def enemyDie(self):
    #Handle enemy death
def nextWave(self):
    #Set up a harder wave
def playerDie(self):
    #Handle player death
def update(self):
    #Check if we should launch a new wave
```

Example 5-20: The methods that will be included in the WaveManager class.

6 Now that we have the shell for the WaveManager class, we need to work with it. In main. py, instantiate a WaveManager before you create a Player object or any Enemy objects.

```
waveManager = WaveManager(3,6)
```

Example 5-21: Instantiate a WaveManager object called *waveManager* in main.py.

```
player = Player("images/Hunter1.bmp", 2,
(25,1,23,23), (0,0,0), waveManager)

for i in range(waveManager.maxWaveSize):
    enemy = Enemy("images/SpacStor.bmp",
1, (101,13,91,59), (69,78,91), screenXY,
player, waveManager)
    gameObjects.append(enemy)
    player.collisionGroup.append(enemy)
```

Example 5-22: Passing *waveManager* as an argument to the Player and Enemy classes.

```
#Update game state
waveManager.update()
for gameObject in gameObjects():
    gameObject.update()
```

Example 5-23: Ensure that *waveManager.update()* runs every frame.

```
def __init__(self, image, scale, clip,
ckey, waveManager):
    self.waveManager = waveManager
```

Example 5-24: The Player class constructor.

```
def __init__(self, image, scale, clip,
ckey, screenXY, gameObjectTarget,
waveManager):
    self.waveManager = waveManager
```

Example 5-25: The Enemy class constructor.

7 We need to use *waveManager* in *player* and the Enemy objects, so pass it in as an argument to the constructors, as shown in example 5-22. Also note another change that we've made: we've modified the **for in** loop to create the Enemy objects so the range is determined by the maximum number of Enemy objects in a wave.

8 The final change that we need to make to main.py is to call the *WaveManager. update()* in our game loop. Include it in the "Update game state" section of the loop, as shown in example 5-23.

9 Now we need to build the links between the Enemy and Player classes and the WaveManager class. In their constructors, add the *waveManager* parameter and set the value of *self.waveManager* to *waveManager*. Examples 5-23 and 5-24 show this.

10 There is less to be done in the Player class, so we will finish that first. When our player dies we want to let *waveManager* know so that it can reset the game state accordingly. The player ship dies in *Player. checkForCollisions()* if there is a collision, call *self.waveManager. playerDie()*, as in example 5-26.

11 In the WaveManager class we will determine what happens when the player dies. In *WaveManager.playerDie()* we want to reset the size of the incoming waves, reset the wave counter, and reset the number of enemies who are active. We will also use a flag, *isActive*, in the Enemy class when enemies are active. We should reset that flag for every Enemy object when the player dies. Example 5-27 shows *WaveManager.playerDie()*.

12 The bulk of progression management will deal with the Enemy object. In the Enemy constructor, append the Enemy object to *waveManager. enemyList* and add the *self. isActive* flag. Initialize the flag to False, as shown in example 5-28.

```
def checkForCollisions(self):
    for gameObject in
self.collisionGroup:
        self.collision =
self.rect.colliderect(gameObject.rect)
        if self.collision:
            self.onDeath()
            for gameObject in
self.collisionGroup:
                gameObject.onDeath()
            self.waveManager.playerDie()
            break
```

Example 5-26: Call *self.waveManager.playerDie()* in the *Player. checkForCollisions()* method.

```
def playerDie(self):
    #Handle player death
    self.waveSize = self.initWaveSize
    self.currentWave = 0
    self.activeNumber = 0
    for enemy in self.enemyList:
     enemy.isActive = False
```

Example 5-27: Have *WaveManager.playerDie()* reset the appropriate game progess variables and ensure that all Enemy objects are not active.

```
    self.waveManager = waveManager
    self.waveManager.enemyList.append(self)
    self.isActive = False
```

Example 5-28: In the Enemy class constructor, add the Enemy object to the *WaveManager.enemyList* array and then set the *self.isActive* flag to False.

13 We initialize our Enemy objects as not active so that they will not move until *waveManager* tells them to. To implement this, in *Enemy.update()* add an **elif** before the **else** statement that processes physics. Have this **elif** check the *self.isActive* flag and, if the Enemy object is not active, zero out the velocities. See example 5-29.

```
    ...
elif not self.isActive:
    self.velocityX = 0
    self.velocityY = 0
else:
    #Check states
    ...
```

Example 5-29: An object that is not active should not be able to move, so implement this in the *Enemy.update()* method.

14 Continuing through the Enemy class, think about when we would want an active Enemy to become inactive. The object would become inactive after the player is killed, but we've already handled that situation. The other circumstance would be when the object is out of bounds. Create a new method named *Enemy.checkBounds()* and call it where you currently check the object's location. In the function, check the Enemy object location. If it is off screen, set *self.isActive* to False and call *self.onDeath()*. Refer to example 5-30. Note that we only want to allow an Enemy object to be out of bounds if it is not chasing the player, and we also only want to check its bounds if it is active.

```
def checkBounds(self):
    if self.state != 2 and self.isActive
and (self.rect.x >= self.rect.width +
self.screenX or self.rect.y >= self.
rect.height + self.screenY):
        self.isActive = False
        self.onDeath()
```

Example 5-30: An enemy will be set to inactive if it goes off of the screen and if it is not chasing the player.

15 The final piece of the Enemy class is to tell *waveManager* that an Enemy object has died. In *Enemy.onDeath()*, call *self.waveManager.enemyDie()*, as shown in example 5-31.

```
def onDeath(self):
    self.waveManager.enemyDie()
    self.isWaitingToRespawn = True
    self.respawnTimer =
playerRespawnTimer
```

Example 5-31: The Enemy class uses *self.waveManager. enemyDie()* to report that it has been destroyed.

16 Now we're ready to dive into the WaveManager class. *WaveManager.activateEnemies()* sets the *isActive* flag on the objects stored in *self.enemyList* to active. It should only activate *self.waveSize* number of enemies and it should only iterate on enemies that are not currently active. Once an enemy is activated, increment *self.activeNumber* to keep track of how many enemies are currently in play. Refer to example 5-32.

```
def activateEnemies(self):
    #Set enemies to active
    for enemy in self.enemyList:
     if self.activeNumber < self.waveSize
and not enemy.isActive:
            enemy.isActive = True
            self.activeNumber += 1
```

Example 5-32: Set the objects in *WaveManager.enemyList* to active until the wave is full.

17 When enemies activate, we increment *self.activeNumber*, so when they die we will decrement the same variable. Do that in *WaveManager.enemyDie()*, as in example 5-33.

```
def enemyDie(self):
    #Handle enemy death
    self.activeNumber -= 1
```

Example 5-33: When an Enemy object dies it is no longer active, so the WaveManager class must reflect that.

```
def nextWave(self):
    #Set up a harder wave
    self.activateEnemies()
    self.currentWave += 1
    if self.waveSize < self.maxWaveSize:
     self.waveSize += 1
```

Example 5-34: Launch a new wave of enemies and prepare the following, more challenging wave.

```
def update(self):
    #Check if we should launch a new wave
    if self.activeNumber <= 0:
     self.nextWave()
```

Example 5-35: Keep checking the number of active enemies. If there are no active enemies, it is time to launch a new wave.

18 We have already handled the situation where a player dies, so we can move on to *WaveManager.nextWave()*. This method is called to create the initial wave of enemies and is then called whenever a new, more challenging wave must appear. Its first task is to activate the appropriate number of enemies. Next, it needs to increment the number of waves sent at the player. Finally, it increases the challenge of the upcoming wave by incrementing the number of enemies the player will face, up to the maximum allowable number of enemies. This method is shown in example 5-34.

19 The final piece of the WaveManager class is the *WaveManager.update()* method. This method will activate a new wave of enemies when there are no more active enemies, as in example 5-35.

Did you follow all of that? Good! The WaveManager class is being updated every frame to check how many enemies are actively engaged with the player. If there are no enemies active, then WaveManager creates a new wave and increases the difficulty level up to a cap that we define in our main.py file. At the moment there is no feedback to let the player know how many waves they have completed or how well they are doing, but we will add that in the next chapter.

In our one-screen game, we are limited in how we increase the challenge for a player. Other possibilities could be to increase the speed of enemies, or to increase their size. The core concept is that in order for a game to be compelling and to sustain a player's interest, it must progress in some manner.

Game progression and game state management logic seems complicated because, by necessity, it touches on all aspects of the game. There are many, many ways to organize and structure game progression and our WaveManager class is only one quick example. As you were working through the code you may have conceived of a completely different method to get very similar results. If so, this would be a great opportunity to take some time to implement your ideas and see how they work.

In the next section we are going to add some polish to our game with animations, sound effects, and a scoring system.

```python
class WaveManager():
    def __init__(self, initWaveSize, maxWaveSize):
        self.currentWave = 0
        self.activeNumber = 0
        self.maxWaveSize = maxWaveSize
        self.initWaveSize = initWaveSize
        self.waveSize = self.initWaveSize
        self.enemyList = []

    def activateEnemies(self):
        #Set enemies to active
        for enemy in self.enemyList:
            if self.activeNumber < self.waveSize and not enemy.isActive:
                enemy.isActive = True
                self.activeNumber += 1

    def enemyDie(self):
        #Handle enemy death
        self.activeNumber -= 1

    def nextWave(self):
        #Set up a harder wave
        self.activateEnemies()
        self.currentWave += 1
        if self.waveSize < self.maxWaveSize:
            self.waveSize += 1

    def playerDie(self):
        #Handle player death
        self.waveSize = self.initWaveSize
        self.currentWave = 0
        self.activeNumber = 0
        for enemy in self.enemyList:
            enemy.isActive = False

    def update(self):
        #Check if we should launch a new wave
        if self.activeNumber <= 0:
            self.nextWave()
```

Example 5-36: The complete WaveManager class.

WHAT HAVE YOU LEARNED?

Questions for Review:

1 How can game progression be implemented?

   a Movement to new levels.

   b Story developments.

   c Increasing difficulty.

   d All of the above.

2 What is one of the jobs of the WaveManager class?

   a Crop the graphics assets for the game object sprites.

   b Draw the background image.

   c Check how many enemies are actively engaged with the player.

   d Keep track of player input.

3 Game state management logic needs to deal with very few aspects of a game.

   a True.

   b False.

4 There are many ways of creating progression in game development.

   a True.

   b False.

CHAPTER 05 LAB EXERCISE

In this lab exercise, you'll be expanding upon the game code used in the chapter. You will create another state for the enemy AI. The new state will have our enemies avoid the player if the player is invincible. To simulate invincibility, use the spacebar. If the spacebar is pressed, the player is invincible.

1 Simulate player invincibility:

a) Create an invincibility attribute for the Player class.

b) Hook the attribute to the spacebar, set it to True when the spacebar is pressed and False when it is released.

2 Add the avoid state:

a) If the enemy is chasing the player and the player is invincible, the enemy should go into the avoid state and move away from the player.

b) Edit the structure of the state machine so that the enemy can only enter state 3 (lost chase) when the player is NOT invincible.

Chapter
06

Quickly Bringing a Game Together

Chapter Objectives:

- You will learn how to implement animations in Pygame.
- You will create a system to track player scores.
- You will add sound and music.
- You will understand how small modifications can have a big impact.

6.1 Animations

At this point, we have a game with tuned gameplay mechanics, obstacles to avoid, enemies to engage, and a progressive level of difficulty. The next step is to begin to add a little polish to the game through including animations, sound effects, and a scoring system.

In this chapter we will add animation to make our game more visually interesting and appealing, we will add sound effects to increase immersion and provide feedback, and we will add a scoring system so the player can track their progress.

First we will add animation. Animation is creating the appearance of movement by making incremental changes to successive images and displaying them in sequence. So far, the movement in our game has been handled by changing the position or rotation of a static image, however, in this section we are going to create an explosion animation by displaying a series of frames from an image file in sequence. Our goal will be to have the player ship explode whenever there is a collision.

Open main.py and gameObjects.py. Also, find the file named "explode4.bmp" in the graphics assets you downloaded earlier. We will use that file as the basis for our animation.

1   First, find the "explode4. bmp" file in the /images/ directory that houses your other graphics. It should look like the image in figure 6-1.

2   Check the image s properties. It has the d mensions 145 by 25 and holds six frames. That means that each frame is approximately 24 by 25 pixels.

Figure 6-1: The graphical asset that will form our explosion.

Also, make a note of the background color of the source image. We will have to use **Surface.set_colorkey()** to make it transparent when we use the explosion asset.

We are going to have our Player object explode when it collides with something, so we will need to change *Player.image* to the explosion at the appropriate time. The first thing that we need to do is load our image assets and for that we will use the *imageLoader()* function that we created earlier.

We will load the images in their own method, and because that method needs to execute whenever a Player object is created, we will call it in the class constructor. We also need to be able to iterate through the frames of the animation, so we will have to keep track of the current frame with another attribute.

3 In the Player class, create *Player.loadExplosionAnimation()*. Call that method from the Player class constructor and create the empty method.

```
def loadExplosionAnimation():
    self.explosionFrames = []
    self.explosionCurrentFrame = 0
```

Example 6-1: The attributes that we will need to use our explosion animation.

4 In *Player.loadExplosionAnimation()*, create the *self.explosionFrames* array to hold the animation frames and create the *self.explosionCurrentFrame* attribute, initialized to 0, to store the current animation frame to display. Example 6-1 shows how *Player.loadExplosionAnimation()* should look at this point.

```
def loadExplosionAnimation():
    self.explosionFrames = []
    self.explosionCurrentFrame = 0
    frameWidth = 24
    for i in range(0,6):
      self.explosionFrames.
append(imageLoader("images/explode4.
bmp", 2, (frameWidth*i, 0, frameWidth,
25)))
```

Example 6-2: Player.loadExplosionAnimation().

5 Each frame of the animation is 24 pixels wide and 25 pixels high, so we can use these values to determine what to pass to *imageLoader()*. Create a *frameWidth* variable and set it to 24.

6 Use a **for in** loop to populate *self.explosionFrames* with the animation frames we need. *frameWidth* is used to determine where *imageLoader()* clips the original asset. Example 6-2 demonstrates the now complete *Player. loadExplosionAnimation()*.

Note that we have passed a value of 2 for the scale in *imageLoader()*. Looking at the size of a frame of our animation, 24 by 25, and the size of the Player object's image asset, 23 by 23, we can tell that they are similar enough in size that they should be scaled similarly. When we instantiate *player* in main.py, we pass 2 as the scale, so we use that as the basis for the explosion animation scale.

Figure 6-2 shows the animation frames and their locations in *Player.explosionFrames*.

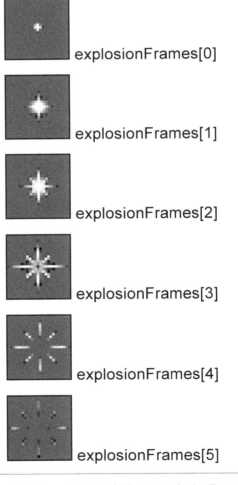

explosionFrames[0]

explosionFrames[1]

explosionFrames[2]

explosionFrames[3]

explosionFrames[4]

explosionFrames[5]

Figure 6-2: The content of *Player.explosionFrames[]*.

```
self.ckey = ckey
self.explosionCkey = (69,78,91)
self.image.set_colorkey(self.ckey)
```

Example 6-3: In the Player class constructor, set the values for the player ship's color key, *self.ckey*, and the explosion animation, *self.explosionCkey*.

```
#Check if object is waiting to respawn
if self.isWaitingToRespawn:
    #Run explosion animation and then
display empty surface
    if self.explosionCurrentFrame < len(-
self.explosionFrames):
        self.image = self.          ex-
plosionFrames[explosionCurrentFrame]
        self.image.set_colorkey(self.explo-
sionCkey)
        self.explosionCurrentFrame += 1
    else:
        self.image =        pygame.
Surface((0,0))
        self.image.set_colorkey(self.ckey)

    ...
```

Example 6-4: The beginning of *Player.update()* with the explosion animation code added.

7 We are almost ready to implement the animation, but we need to prepare two more attributes. In the Player class constructor, assign *self.ckey* to the argument *ckey* so that we can access the Player object's color key value when we reset the Player image. Also, create an attribute *self.explosionCkey* and set it to the RGB value we intend to make transparent for the explosion animation. Example 6-3 shows this part of the class constructor.

8 *Player.update()* is run every frame so we can use that to loop through our animation. If the Player object is waiting to respawn, then it has been destroyed and our explosion animation should play. Play the animation by changing the value of *self.image* to the appropriate frame of the animation and then iterating *self.explosionCurrentFrame*. If all of the animation frames have been played, set *self.image* to an empty Surface object. Example 6-4 shows the appropriate code. Note where we set the appropriate color key of *self.image*.

9 Now that the animation displays the appropriate frame with the appropriate color key and, upon completion, resets the color key for the player ship image, we only have to reset the value of *self. explosionCurrentFrame* to 0 so the animation can play again. Do this in *Player.reset()* when the other important Player object variables are reset, as shown in example 6-5.

```
def reset(self):
    self.rect.x = 400
    self.rect.y = 300
    self.velocityX = 0
    self.velocityY = 0
    self.explosionCurrentFrame = 0
    self.collision = False
    self.isWaitingToRespawn = False
```

Example 6-5: Resetting the value of *self. explosionCurrentFrame* in *Player.reset()* so that the explosion can play more than once.

Now when our player's ship is struck by an enemy, it is destroyed in a nice little explosion.

As the game projects that you work on grow, you'll need to increase the complexity of your animations and you will probably want to set up classes to manage and organize your animation functions. The basic concept of animation in games, though, is simple: select the images that will make up the animation, load them into your game, and loop through them at the appropriate time.

In the next section we will introduce a score and demonstrate a method to keep track of which wave the player is currently facing.

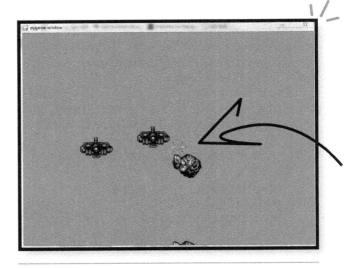

Figure 6-3: An explosion shows when the player's ship is struck.

Questions for Review:

1 What is animation in games?

a Any game designed by a Disney studio.

b Creating a complex skeletal framework and moving it according to realistic biology.

c Creating the appearance of movement by making incremental changes to successive images.

d You cannot have animation in games.

2 What do we need to implement an animation in our game?

a A graphical asset or assets with the animation frames.

b A variable to reference the current animation frame.

c A loop to iterate through the animation frames.

d All of the above.

3 Graphical assets needed for an animation should only be loaded when the animation is going to play.

a True.

b False.

4 There is only one effective way to implement animations in Pygame.

a True.

b False.

6.2 Implementing Scores

In order to reflect the progression that we implemented in chapter five, we are going to create a score display for the player. Pygames has built-in display methods, but because not all computers recognize Pygames fonts, we are going to use a sprite sheet to hold our numbers.

Go to http://goo.gl/i1jKCM and download the assets file, and then find numbers.bmp. Save it in the /images/ folder that houses all of the other image assets we have been using.

The file contains images for the numbers 0 through 9 and each number is 30 pixels wide and 49 pixels high. Using *imageLoader()* these images can be placed into an array that has index values that correspond to the digit, allowing us to easily implement these images as our game's score.

1 In main.py, include imageLoader.py to access the *imageLoader()* function, as shown in example 6-6.

```
from imageLoader import *
```

Example 6-6: Import imageLoader in main.py.

2 Create an array that will store the number images, named *scoreNums*.

3 Create *scoreNumsWidth* and set it to 30.

4 Use a **for in** loop and the known width and height of the numbers to populate *scoreNums* with the appropriate images. Refer to example 6-7.

```
scoreNums = []
scoreNumsWidth = 30
for i in range(0,10):
    scoreNums.append(imageLoader
("images/numbers.bmp",1,(scoreNumsWidth
* i, 0, 30, 49))
```

Example 6-7: Store the number images in an array.

Figure 6-4: The numbers.bmp file.

5 We need to determine what the player's score is, so go to the WaveManager class in gameObjects.py. Create a *WaveManager.score* attribute and initialize it to 0 in the WaveManager constructor.

6 We don't want to increment the score whenever *WaveManager.enemyDie()* is called because that method is called even when the player is killed. Instead, we want to increment the score when an Enemy object is out of bounds. In the Enemy class increment *self.waveManager.score* in the *Enemy.checkBounds()* method, as shown in example 6-8.

```
def checkBounds(self):
    if self.state != 2 and self.isActive
and (self.rect.x >= self.rect.width +
self.screenX or self.rect.y >= self.
rect.height + self.screenY):
        self.isActive = False
        self.waveManager.score += 1
        self.onDeath()
```

Example 6-8: Increment *WaveManager.score* only when you know that the enemy was killed because it went out of bounds. *Enemy.checkBoudnds()* is the best place for this.

Now that we have a score variable that is being incremented to appropriately match the player's score, we need to get each individual digit from that value. We will do this using the modulus operator. Modulus returns the remainder of a division operation.

If we want to get the ones digit in the number 27 we would perform the operation "27 % 10." The division of 27 by 10 would result in 2 with a remainder of 7. In order to get the tens digit in the number 27 we would perform the operation "27 % 100." The division of 27 by 100 would result in 0 with a remainder of 27. In order to only return the tens digit, we would subtract the value of the ones digit, which we know to be 7, and then divide by 10. 27 minus 7 is 20, and 20 divided by 10 is 2.

```
firstDigit = waveManager.score % 10
secondDigit = (waveManager.score % 100 -
firstDigit) / 10
thirdDigit = (waveManager.score % 1000 -
firstDigit - secondDigit) / 100
```

Example 6-9: Use modulus to determine the value of the digits of *waveManager.score*.

We need the score to display on top of every other element, so we will **blit()** it to *screen* just before we call **pygame.display.flip()**.

7 In the main game loop of main.py, after having displayed the game updates but before **pygame.display. flip()**, determine the three digits of the player's score using the modulus operator, as shown in example 6-9.

```
screen.blit(scoreNums[firstDigit],
(64,0))
screen.blit(scoreNums[secondDigit],
(32,0))
screen.blit(scoreNums[thirdDigit],
(0,0))
```

Example 6-10: The number images in *scoreNums* correspond to the index values, so we can display the appropriate numbers easily.

8 To display those digits, use *screen.blit()*. When positioning the surfaces remember that each image is 30 pixels wide, so if *thirdDigit* is in the top left, *secondDigit* and *firstDigit* must both be offset. Example 6-10 shows the score display code.

Now, when you play your game, you'll see a score counter increment in the upper left-hand corner of the screen!

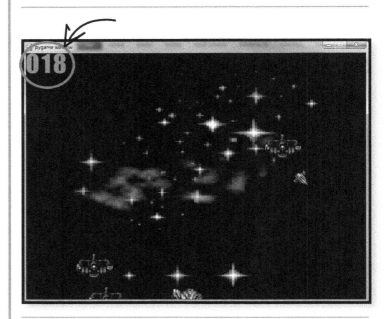

Figure 6-5: The score is shown on the screen!

```
#Display Wave
waveDisplayX = screenXY[0] -
scoreNumsWidth
firstDigitWave = waveManager.currentWave
% 10
secondDigitWave = (waveManager.
currentWave % 100 - firstDigitWave) / 10
thirdDigitWave = (waveManager.
currentWave % 1000 - firstDigitWave -
secondDigitWave) / 100
screen.blit(scoreNums[firstDigitWave],
(waveDisplayX,0))
screen.blit(scoreNums[secondDigitWave],
(waveDisplayX - 32,0))
screen.blit(scoreNums[thirdDigitWave],
(waveDisplayX - 64,0))
```

Example 6-11: The code to display wave information in the upper right-hand corner of the screen.

Figure 6-6: Now both the score and the wave number are displayed!

It's important to display the score, but it would also be good to keep track of which wave the player is currently engaged with. For this, we only need to access the value of *waveManager.currentWave* and display it in the same manner we have displayed the score in.

9 Using steps 7 and 8 as a reference, in the upper right-hand side of the screen display the wave number that the player is currently engaged with. Example 6-11 shows how your wave display code should look.

In this section we have implemented scoring to keep track of a player's progress through the game, and also introduced a wave counter to let the player know how many waves of enemies they have moved through. This was all done in the main.py file, however, this could have been a good candidate for a function associated with a more robust game manager. Our simple WaveManager class already held much of the data that we needed when implementing a scoring system, so expanding on that class would allow us to create a more robust scoring system.

This chapter made it clear how valuable it is to have the progression management in place. When we implemented WaveManager, we had to create the code that connected it to our game objects in a number of different places. Once that was implemented, though, it was easy to use the information that WaveManager was already storing to give our players real feedback on their progress through the game.

In the next section we will add sounds to the game to provide even more feedback to our player.

```
import pygame, sys
from gameObjects import *
from imageLoader import *
pygame.init()
#Create the application window
screenXY = (800,600)
screen = pygame.display.set_mode(screenXY)

#Create the game objects
gameObjects = []
waveManager = WaveManager(3,6)
background = Background(
                "images/Nebula1.bmp",screen.get_width(),
                screen.get_height()
                )
player = Player("images/Hunter1.bmp",2,(25,1,23,23),(0,0,0),waveManager)
gameObjects.append(player)
for i in range(5):
    asteroid = Asteroid("images/Rock2a.bmp",1,(6,3,80,67),(69,78,91),screenXY)
    gameObjects.append(asteroid)
    #player.collisionGroup.append(asteroid)
for i in range(waveManager.maxWaveSize):
    enemy = Enemy(
            "images/SpacStor.bmp",1,(101,13,91,59),(69,78,91),screenXY,
            player,waveManager
            )
    gameObjects.append(enemy)
    player.collisionGroup.append(enemy)

scoreNums = []
scoreNumsWidth = 30
for i in range(0,10):
    scoreNums.append(imageLoader("images/numbers.bmp",1,
(scoreNumsWidth*i,0,30,49)))

#Create the game clock
clock = pygame.time.Clock()
```

```
#The game loop
while True:
    for event in pygame.event.get():
     if event.type == pygame.QUIT:
            pygame.quit()
    #Update WaveManager
    waveManager.update()
    #Update game state
    for gameObject in gameObjects:
     gameObject.update()
    #Display game updates
    if player.collision:
     screen.fill((255,0,0))
    else:
     screen.blit(background.image, (background.rect.x,background.rect.y))
     for gameObject in gameObjects:
      screen.blit(gameObject.image, (gameObject.rect.x, gameObject.rect.y))
#Display Score
firstDigit = waveManager.score % 10
secondDigit = (waveManager.score % 100 - firstDigit) / 10
thirdDigit = (waveManager.score % 1000 - firstDigit - secondDigit) / 100
screen.blit(scoreNums[firstDigit], (64,0) )
screen.blit(scoreNums[secondDigit], (32,0) )
screen.blit(scoreNums[thirdDigit], (0,0) )
#Display Wave
waveDisplayX = screenXY[0] - scoreNumsWidth
firstDigitWave = waveManager.currentWave % 10
secondDigitWave = (waveManager.currentWave % 100 - firstDigitWave) / 10
thirdDigitWave = (waveManager.currentWave % 1000 - firstDigitWave -
secondDigitWave) / 100
screen.blit(scoreNums[firstDigitWave], (waveDisplayX,0))
screen.blit(scoreNums[secondDigitWave], (waveDisplayX - 32,0))
screen.blit(scoreNums[thirdDigitWave], (waveDisplayX - 64,0))
pygame.display.flip()
clock.tick(60)
```

Example 6-12: The complete main.py file.

Questions for Review:

1 What is a good reason to implement scores in a game?

    a To reflect player progression.

    b To give the player a sense of accomplishment.

    c To allow the player to track their skill in the game.

    d All of the above.

2 In our game loop, when should we display the score?

    a At the start of every game loop.

    b At the end of every game loop.

    c Before drawing any other game elements.

    d Just before **pygame.display.flip()**.

3 What is the purpose of displaying the current wave?

    a To have a multiple that can be applied to the score.

    b To make the screen appear more symmetrical.

    c To reinforce player progression.

    d There is no point to displaying the current wave.

4 The score logic could be included in a more robust game manager.

    a True.

    b False.

6.3 Adding Sound

In this section we are going to add some sound effects and music to our game. Adding sound files to your Pygame project and using them is very simple. In this game, we're going to use the audio files that were included in the file you downloaded in the previous section from http://goo.gl/i1jKCM

The files are named explosion.wav, music.wav, and next-wave.wav. Extract them and place them in an /audio/ folder in your main Pygames project directory.

We will use explosion.wav when the player ship is destroyed, next-wave.wav to let the player know that they have advanced to a new wave of enemies, and music.wav as background music. First, we will load these files in main.py.

1 In main.py, immediately after calling **pygame.init()**, create three sound objects named *music*, *explosion*, and *nextWave*. Assign them the values of the audio files you have just extracted. Example 6-13 shows you how this is done.

```
music = pygame.mixer.Sound("audio/music.
wav")
explosion = pygame.mixer.Sound("audio/
explosion.wav")
nextWave = pygame.mixer.Sound("audio/
next-wave.wav")
```

Example 6-13: Initialize Sound objects using the audio files as arguments.

2 You can play any of these files using the *.play()* method. If you pass the -1 argument to *.play()* then the file will loop endlessly. Test this with each file in turn.

```
music.play(-1)
```

Example 6-14: Loop the background music file to test it. You may want to comment this code out to test the other sound files.

3 If you like, you can set *music.play()* to loop immediately after it is initialized, as in example 6-14.

```
waveManager = WaveManager(3,6,nextWave)
player = Player("images/Hunter1.bmp", 2,
(25,1,23,23), (0,0,0), waveManager,
explosion)
```

Example 6-15: Pass *nextWave* and *explosion* to *waveManager* and *player*, respectively, as arguments.

```
def __init__(self, image, scale, clip,
ckey, waveManager, explosionSound):
    ...
    self.explosionSound = explosionSound
    ...
```

Example 6-16: Insert *self.explosionSound = explosionSound* into the Player class constructor.

```
def __init__(self, initWaveSize,
maxWaveSize, nextWaveSound):
    ...
    self.nextWaveSound = nextWaveSound
    ...
```

Example 6-17: Insert *self.nextWaveSound = nextWaveSound* into the WaveManager class constructor.

```
def onDeath(self):
    self.isWaitingToRespawn = True
    self.respawnTimer =
playerRespawnTimer
    self.explosionSound.play()
```

Example 6-18: Play the explosion sound effect when the player's ship is destroyed.

It is probably a good idea to comment out the *music.play(-1)* line while testing the other sound effects.

4 *explosion* is going to be passed as an argument to the Player object, and *nextWave* will be passed as an argument to the WaveManager object, as in exmple 6-15.

5 In the Player class constructor, add a parameter for *explosionSound* and initialize *self.explosionSound* to *explosionSound*.

6 In the WaveManager class constructor, do the same as step 5 for a parameter *nextWaveSound*. Examples 6-16 and 6-17 show the sound parameters in the Player and WaveManager class constructors.

7 In *Player.onDeath()*, play *self.explosionSound* using *self.explosionSound.play()* as in example 6-18.

In the WaveManager class, we will play the *nextWaveSound* file only when there is a new wave of enemies, *not* when it is the first wave of the game or the first wave after a player has died.

8   In *WaveManager.nextWave()*, check if the value of *self.currentWave* is higher than 1 and if it is, then play the *self.nextWaveSound* file, as shown in example 6-19.

```python
def nextWave(self):
    self.activateEnemies()
    self.currentWave += 1
    if self.currentWave > 1:
     self.nextWaveSound.play()
    if self.waveSize < self.maxWaveSize:
     self.waveSize += 1
```

Example 6-19: Play the sound effect for a new enemy wave when the player has advanced to a new wave, not when the game begins or when the player dies.

Now you can remove the comment from *music.play(-1)* in main.py and play your game, complete with music, sound effects, score, progression, and enemy AI!

In the final section we will demonstrate how much a game can be changed by making minor tweaks to a few attributes and values.

Questions for Review:

1 What is one reason to add sound effects and music to a game?

    a To keep the player from falling asleep at the keyboard.

    b To reinforce gameplay events.

    c To expose the reader to new types of music.

    d There is no reason to add sound effects and music to a game.

2 Which sound elements should have the value of "-1" passed as an argument to their **.play()** method?

    a Background music.

    b Explosion sound effects.

    c Character dialogue.

    d All of the above.

3 Appropriate sound and music have little effect on a final product.

    a True.

    b False.

4 Sounds can be used as rewards in a game.

    a True.

    b False.

6.4 Modifying Your Game

Now the basic mechanics of your space game are complete. A player's score is tracked, there are enemies to avoid, there is a sense of progression, and there is sound. The game is not complete, however. In this final section, you will learn how to adjust the game that we've been developing in order to make it your own.

We'll make a few small tweaks to show you how easy it is to change the feeling and playability of your game using the framework that we have already developed. When you move on and begin developing your own games, it's important to keep in mind that small, evolutionary changes to individual gameplay elements can combine to result in tremendous change to the final product. We'll make a number of such changes here and recommend further changes that you can make on your own.

The first change that we are going to make is to re-enable collision with the Asteroid obstacles. Ensure that gameObjects.py and main.py are both open.

1 In main.py, find the **for in** loop that instantiates the Asteroid objects. The code that appends the Asteroid objects to *player.collisionGroup* is commented out, so remove the comment so that the player will have to avoid asteroids as well as enemies. Example 6-20 shows the correct **for in** loop.

```
for i in range(5):
    asteroid = Asteroid("images/
Rock2a.bmp", 1, (6,3,80,67), (69,78,91),
screenXY)
    gameObjects.append(asteroid)
    player.collisionGroup.append(
asteroid)
```

Example 6-20: Asteroids implemented as a collidable obstacle again.

2 When you run the game you'll probably discover an immediate problem — the game, with the current Asteroid objects, is very challenging. Probably too challenging.

Creating the proper challenge level for a game is a major part of game development. Our game only features obstacles and enemies, and we have already tuned the action of our enemies. To create a more reasonable challenge for the player while still adding the asteroid obstacles, we will use the physics framework we built in the Asteroid class to reduce the speed of incoming asteroids. Ensure that you are working on gameObjects.py and follow along with the following steps.

3 Go to the Asteroid class in gameObjects.py and check the value of *self.velocityX* and *self.velocityY*.

4 Recall that acceleration is not used for our Asteroid objects, so we only need to modify their velocity values. Change *self.velocityX* and *self.velocityY* to a lower value, like 3. This is shown in example 6-21.

```
self.velocityX = 3
self.velocityY = 3
```

Example 6-21: Setting the velocity attributes in the Asteroid class to a more reasonable value.

```
randomVel = random.randrange(2,5)
self.velocityX = randomVel
self.velocityY = randomVel
```

Example 6-22: Introducing some randomness to the speed of the Asteroid objects.

5 Once you've saved gameObjects.py, test the game and consider how the movement of the asteroid obstacles feels. If you think that it needs further tuning, continue modifying the class's velocity attributes.

6 Also recall the **random. randrange()** method. Example 6-22 demonstrates using it to provide variety to the asteroids' velocities.

Now we have collidable asteroids that move at a reasonable pace. The player has a further challenge in avoiding collisions with the asteroid obstacles, but they are traveling slowly enough to be a fair challenge. We have also introduced a little randomness into the velocity of the asteroids to make the game more interesting.

We can further increase the variety of the obstacles by changing their size. When creating the *imageLoader()* function we included a *scale* parameter. We had used this to increase the size of the player, but we can also use it to create variety in the size of Asteroid objects.

```
for i in range(5):
    asteroid = Asteroid("images/
Rock2a.bmp", random.randrange(1,3),
(6,3,80,67), (69,78,91), screenXY)
    gameObjects.append(asteroid)
    player.collisionGroup.append
(asteroid)
```

Example 6-23: Asteroid instantiation with random sizes implemented.

7 In main.py, return to the **for in** loop that instantiates the Asteroid objects.

8 When each Asteroid object is being created, pass a random range of values in place of the static scale. Example 6-23 demonstrates this code.

9 When you play the game, note how gameplay feels different when the obstacle size and velocity are randomized. It should feel much more dynamic now.

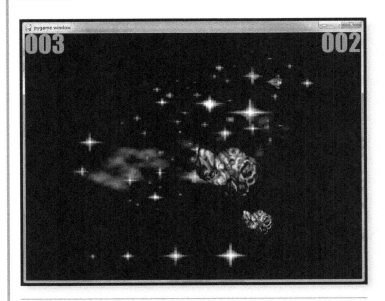

Figure 6-7: Now Asteroid objects have different sizes!

```
player = Player("images/Hunter1.bmp", 1,
(25,1,23,23), (0,0,0), waveManager,
explosion)
```

Example 6-24: Implementing a smaller Player object.

One final change that we will make is to the size of the player's ship. Instead of increasing the scale or introducing randomness, as we did with the Asteroid objects, we will reduce the size of the player.

10 In main.py, when the player is instantiated, set the value of the scale argument to one, as shown in example 6-24.

11 When you play the game, think about how having a much smaller player ship changes how the game feels. You might think that a smaller object representing the player will make them feel less powerful, but the smaller hitbox makes it easier to avoid obstacles so the player may instead feel *more* powerful.

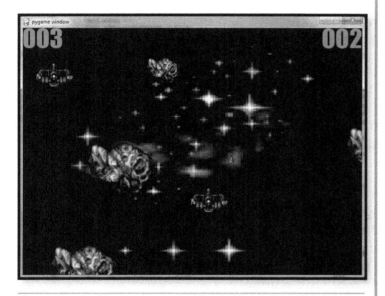

Figure 6-8: The game with a smaller player has a very different feeling.

Playing the game now, with only these few changes made, is a very different experience.

Further modifications and enhancements can take even this simple game in different directions. You could increase the speed or maneuverability of enemy ships as the waves increase, or introduce power ups that change the attributes of the player's ship. One of the best ways to fine tune your game is to have other people play it, and use their feedback to determine what changes you need to make.

Congratulations! By following along with the exercises and examples in this book, you've created a fully functioning space action game!

In this book, you've gained some of the key skills required of any game developer. You have learned how to create and use a game loop, you have gained an understanding of how to create game objects from raw assets, you have learned how to implement game logic, object logic, and event logic, you have been exposed to artificial intelligence, and you have learned how to implement a game state manager that tracks player progress.

Most importantly, you've learned how much detail goes into creating the unique feeling of a game, and how even small changes to the mechanics behind the scenes can affect the experience a player has. Much has been made of the question of artistry in games. There is undeniably art in the myriad assets that are used in the creation of the graphics, sounds, and narratives for games, however, there is also artistry in the creation of the mechanics of games. Creating a compelling experience for a player is challenging, but a solid foundational understanding of game development concepts is the most important step in designing a game for any language.

Thank you for reading...now get out there and make some games!

Questions for Review:

1 Small changes to the game mechanics will only ever have a small change on the gameplay.

    a True.

    b False.

2 What change would have no impact on gameplay?

    a Increasing the speed of enemies.

    b Introducing asteroids that travel in a different direction.

    c Increasing the size of the player ship.

    d None of the above.

3 What is the best way to fine tune your game?

    a Play it yourself and make the changes that you know are correct.

    b Release a video of the game being played on YouTube, and base any changes on the whims of YouTube commenters.

    c Have people you trust play the game and seriously consider their feedback.

    d You do not need to fine tune your game.

4 Which of the following do you need to create good games? (Choose all that apply)

    a Practice.

    b Patience.

    c Determination.

    d A cat.

CHAPTER 06 LAB EXERCISE

In this lab exercise, we'll be adding another animation: thrust. Adding thrust is a little more complicated than adding an explosion, since the boundaries of the thrust and the player extend past the original dimensions of the assets, and the thrust and ship assets should be merged into one asset for drawing.

1 Load in the thrust animation frames:

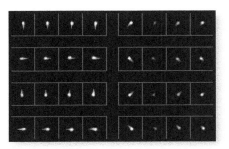

a) Load in the thrust frames using the Exhaust1. bmp file from the graphics asset pack you have downloaded. It's a good idea to only use the top right four frames and rotate the asset with the ship. It's also a good idea to scale it appropriately to the size of the player.

b) Implement a current frame variable. Increment the frame counter each frame. If the count is greater than the number of frames, reset it.

2 Draw the thrust:

a) **blit()** the thrust to the player asset before it is rotated. It's a good idea to rotate both assets together at the same time.

b) Position the thrust correctly towards the bottom of the ship. You will need to create a new surface, since the thrust and the ship is larger than the original boundaries. Once you've created a new surface, blit both assets to the new surface.

c) Make sure the ship is drawn on top.

d) **blit()** the thrust only when the player is thrusting.

ANSWER KEY

Chapter 01

Section 1.1

1. What is a game loop?

  A. The pattern of receiving player input, updating the game, and then rendering the updates.

2. In an RGB color value, what does the "G" stand for?

  C. Green.

3. The following is a valid RGB value: (0,134,265)

  B. False.

4. What are Frames Per Second in video games?

  D. The number of times the game is rendered each second.

Section 1.2

1. What is the Event Queue?

  C. The list of player inputs stored as an event object.

2. In Pygame, where is the origin position of a surface located?

  B. The top left pixel.

3. What does **pygame.key. get_pressed()** return?

  D. An array with the boolean value of every key on the keyboard.

4. In order to ensure that the background renders appropriately, it must be rendered before any other element.

  A. True.

Section 1.3

1. How do you keep track of time in Pygame?

  A. pygame.time.get_ticks()

2. Why is it important to consider optimizations in your game?

  D. All of the above.

3. What is the most straightforward way to avoid lag?

  C. Do less work per game loop.

4. What is a good target frame rate for modern games?

B. 60.

Chapter 02

Section 2.1

1. What is a surface in Pygame?

B. An object that is used to represent any image.

2. What does the width parameter of **pygame.draw.circle()** do?

C. Defines the width of the line that draws the circle.

3. When drawing to a surface, what is the origin of the location coordinates for the source surface?

C. The origin of the target surface.

4. What does **pygame. Surface.blit()** do?

A. Draws one surface on to another surface.

Section 2.2

1. What should you keep in mind when creating your game?

C. Placeholder graphics that may not exactly match your vision are very useful when developing core gameplay concepts.

2. What does **pygame. transform.scale()** do?

A. Takes a surface argument and returns a new surface that is a scaled version of the source surface.

3. You can use **pygame.surface.blit()** to crop out a part of the source surface.

A. True.

4. Transform operations in Pygame never return a surface.

B. False.

Section 2.3

1. What does pygame.transform. laplacian() return?

B. Basic edge detection of a surface.

2. How can we access the color data from individual pixels of a surface?

C. By accessing the pixel array with pygame.PixelArray().

3. What is a hex triplet?

C. A three byte hexadecimal number which correlates to an RGB value.

4. A surface can be created from a pixel array.

A. True.

Section 2.4

1. What are sprites?

D. 2D images that are a part of a larger scene and that can be manipulated without modifying the overall scene.

2. When extending the Sprite class, why is it useful to include *self.rect* attribute?

C. Because Pygame's Sprite class has methods that use the *self.rect* attribute.

3. The Sprite class should only be used for player controlled objects.

B. False.

4. The Sprite class has built-in methods that can be useful when designing in Pygame.

A. True.

Chapter 03

Section 3.1

1. What do Pong and Star Citizen have in common?

C. Both games are simulations that use a physics engine.

2. What is the simplest way to create movement in a 2D game?

B. Change the x and y coordinates of objects in every frame.

3. Why is it useful to use acceleration?

A. To increase velocity in every loop iteration.

4. The update() method of our objects is intended to hold all of the code that we want updated in each frame.

A. True.

Section 3.2

1. What is the first thing to consider when creating player input?

C. What we want our player to be able to do.

2. How do we use the values returned from **pygame.key.get_pressed()**?

C. Store them in an array to be processed later.

3. What does **pygame.transform.rotate()** return?

A. A new surface scaled to fit the rotated source surface.

4. There is no need to maintain an unmodified version of a rotated game asset.

B. False.

Section 3.3

1. What is thrust?

D. A reaction force that accelerates a system.

2. What does our damping force do?

D. All of the above.

3. There is no good reason to modify the values of thrust and damping used in this chapter.

B. False.

4. The best way to create a gameplay experience that matches your goals is through experimentation and testing.

A. True.

Section 3.4

1. What is collision detection?

C. Determining if an object is in contact with another object.

2. What are the collision boxes that enclose a game element called?

D. Bounding box.

3. More precise collision detection is more processor intensive.

A. True.

4. Using hitboxes, or bounding boxes, is a very precise method of collision detection.

B. False.

Chapter 04

Section 4.1

1. What is game object logic?

A. Game logic that controls certain game objects.

2. Why do we call *Asteroid. reset()* at the end of the Asteroid class constructor?

C. In order to call the reset() method, the method that appropriately positions our Asteroid objects.

3. Multiplying the positive x and y coordinates of an Asteroid object by -1 positions the object below and to the right of the game screen.

B. False.

4. What is the best way to create endless waves of asteroid obstacles?

D. Reuse Asteroid objects by calling the *Asteroid.reset()* function when they move off screen.

Section 4.2

1. What is event logic?

C. Code that is executed when certain game events occur.

2. What is a useful starting point when creating a *reset()* method?

C. The values in the class constructor that may change during play.

3. Using the *Player.collisionGroup* array lets us call the *onDeath()* method of every collidable object in the game.

A. True.

4. Event logic allows us to ensure certain events happen in every iteration of the game loop.

B. False.

Section 4.3

1. What is a good reason to delay game events?

A. To make the game less jarring for a player.

2. In a game running at 60 frames per second, how many seconds is 180 ticks?

A. 2.

3. In our game, we only need to implement a delay for the Player class.

B. False.

4. What do we use to create delays?

A. Flagging variables and timer variables.

Chapter 05

Section 5.1

1. What is artificial intelligence in video games?

B. The intelligent behavior of non-playable characters.

2. What is a vector?

D. A way to describe movement from one point in space to another.

3. In order to use vectors in our AI programming, we need to normalize them.

A. True.

4. What do we use as the basis for acceleration in the Enemy class physics?

A. Target vectors.

Section 5.2

1. What is a state machine?

A. An abstract machine that can be in one of a set number of states.

2. What is the term for a change between one state and another state in a state machine?

C. Transition.

3. How many states can a state machine have?

D. There is no hard limit.

4. Is a vending machine an example of a state machine?

A. Yes.

Section 5.3

1. How can game progression be implemented?

D. All of the above.

2. What is one of the jobs of the WaveManager class?

C. Check how many enemies are actively engaged with the player.

3. Game state management logic needs to deal with very few aspects of a game.

B. False.

4. There are many ways of creating progression in game development.

A. True.

Chapter 06

Section 6.1

1. What is animation in games?

C. Creating the appearance of movement by making incremental changes to successive images.

2. What do we need to implement an animation in our game?

D. All of the above.

3. Graphical assets needed for an animation should only be loaded when the animation is going to play.

B. False.

4. There is only one effective way to implement animations in Pygame.

B. False.

Section 6.2

1. What is a good reason to implement scores in a game?

D. All of the above.

2. In our game loop, when should we display the score?

D. Just before **pygame.display.flip()**.

3. What is the purpose of displaying the current wave?

C. To reinforce player progression.

4. The score logic could be included in a more robust game manager.

A. True.

Section 6.3

1. What is one reason to add sound effects and music to a game?

B. To reinforce gameplay events.

2. Which sound elements should have the value of "-1" passed as an argument to their **.play()** method?

   A. Background music.

3. Appropriate sound and music have little effect on a final product.

   B. False.

4. Sounds can be used as rewards in a game.

   A. True.

4. Which of the following do you need to create good games? (Choose all that apply)

   A. Practice.

   B. Patience.

   C. Determination.

Section 6.4

1. Small changes to the game mechanics will only ever have a small change on the gameplay.

   B. False.

2. What change would have no impact on gameplay?

   D. None of the above.

3. What is the best way to fine tune your game?

   C. Have people you trust play the game and seriously consider their feedback.

Appendix A

main.py

```python
import pygame, sys, random
from gameObjects import *
from imageLoader import *

pygame.init()

music = pygame.mixer.Sound("audio/music.wav")
explosion = pygame.mixer.Sound("audio/explosion.wav")
nextWave = pygame.mixer.Sound("audio/next-wave.wav")
# Uncomment the following line to loop the background music
# music.play(-1)

# Create the application window
screenXY = (800, 600)
screen = pygame.display.set_mode(screenXY)

# Create the game objects
gameObjects = []
waveManager = WaveManager(3, 6, nextWave)
background = Background("images/Nebula1.bmp", screen.get_width(),
screen.get_height())
player = Player("images/Hunter1.bmp", 1, (25, 1, 23, 23), (0, 0,
0), waveManager, explosion)
gameObjects.append(player)

for i in range(5):
    # Create the Asteroid obstacles
    asteroid = Asteroid("images/Rock2a.bmp", random.randrange(1,
3), (6, 3, 80, 67), (69, 78, 91), screenXY)
    gameObjects.append(asteroid)
    player.collisionGroup.append(asteroid)
```

```python
    for i in range(waveManager.maxWaveSize):
        # Create the Enemies
        enemy = Enemy("images/SpacStor.bmp", 1, (101, 13, 91, 59),
    (69, 78, 91), screenXY, player, waveManager)
        gameObjects.append(enemy)
        player.collisionGroup.append(enemy)

    scoreNums = []
    scoreNumsWidth = 30
    for i in range(0, 10):
        scoreNums.append(imageLoader("images/numbers.bmp", 1,
    (scoreNumsWidth * i, 0, 30, 49)))

    # Create the game clock
    clock = pygame.time.Clock()

    # The game loop
    while True:
        for event in pygame.event.get():
          if event.type == pygame.QUIT:
                pygame.quit()

        # Update WaveManager
        waveManager.update()

        # Update the game state
        for gameObject in gameObjects:
         gameObject.update()

        # Display the game updates
        if player.collision:
         screen.fill( (255, 0, 0))
        else:
         screen.blit(background.image, (background.rect.x, background.
    rect.y))
        for gameObject in gameObjects:
          screen.blit(gameObject.image, (gameObject.rect.x, gameObject.
    rect.y))
```

```
    # Display score
    firstDigit = waveManager.score % 10
    secondDigit = (waveManager.score % 100 - firstDigit) / 10
    thirdDigit = (waveManager.score % 1000 - firstDigit -
secondDigit) / 100
    screen.blit(scoreNums[firstDigit], (64, 0))
    screen.blit(scoreNums[secondDigit], (32, 0))
    screen.blit(scoreNums[thirdDigit], (0, 0))

    # Display wave
    waveDisplayX = screenXY[0] - scoreNumsWidth
    firstDigitWave = waveManager.currentWave % 10
    secondDigitWave = (waveManager.currentWave % 100 - firstDigit)
/ 10
    thirdDigitWave = (waveManager.currentWave % 1000 - firstDigit -
secondDigit) / 100
    screen.blit(scoreNums[firstDigitWave], (waveDisplayX, 0))
    screen.blit(scoreNums[secondDigitWave], (waveDisplayX - 32,
0))
    screen.blit(scoreNums[thirdDigitWave], (waveDisplayX - 64, 0))

    pygame.display.flip()
    clock.tick(60)
```

imageLoader.py

```python
import pygame

def imageLoader(image, scale, clip):
    asset = pygame.image.load(image)
    assetClipped = pygame.Surface( (clip[2], clip[3]))
    assetClipped.blit(asset, (0, 0), clip)
    return pygame.transform.scale(assetClipped, (clip[2] * scale,
clip[3] * scale))
```

Appendix B

gameObjects.py

```python
import pygame, random, math
from imageLoader import *

playerRespawnTimer = 120 # Ticks

class Background(pygame.sprite.Sprite):
    def __init__(self, image, width, height):
      self.originalAsset = pygame.image.load(image)
      self.image = pygame.transform.scale(self.originalAsset, (width,
height))
      self.rect = self.rect.image.get_rect()
    def update(self):
      return

class Player(pygame.sprite.Sprite):
    def __init__(self, image, scale, clip, ckey, waveManager,
explosionSound):
        self.asset = imageLoader(image, scale, clip)
        self.image = self.asset
        self.ckey = ckey
        self.explosionCkey = (69, 78, 91)
        self.image.set_colorkey(self.ckey)
        self.rect = self.image.get_rect()
        self.rect.x = 400
        self.rect.y = 300
        self.velocityX = 0
        self.velocityY = 0
        self.maxVelocity = 8
        self.accelerationX = 0
        self.accelerationY = 0
        self.thrust = 0.5
        self.damping = 0.3
        self.angle = 0
        self.collision = False
        self.collisionGroup = []
        self.isWaitingToRespawn = False
        self.respawnTimer = 0
        self.waveManager = waveManager
        self.loadExplosionAnimation()
```

```
        self.explosionSound = explosionSound
        self.onSpawn()

    def loadExplosionAnimation(self):
        self.explosionFrames = []
        self.explosionCurrentFrame = 0
        frameWidth = 24
        for i in range(0, 6):
            self.explosionFrames.append(imageLoader("images/explode4.
bmp", 2, (frameWidth + i, 0, frameWidth, 25)))

    def onSpawn(self):
        self.reset()

    def onDeath(self):
        self.isWaitingToRespawn = True
        self.respawnTimer = playerRespawnTimer
        self.explosionSound.play()

    def reset(self):
        self.rect.x = 400
        self.rect.y = 300
        self.velocityX = 0
        self.velocityY = 0
        self.explosionCurrentFrame = 0
        self.collision = False
        self.isWaitingToRespawn = False

    def update(self):
        # Check if the object is waiting to respawn
        if self.isWaitingToRespawn:
            # Run explosion animation
            if self.explosionCurrentFrame < len(self.explosionFrames):
                self.image = self.explosionFrames[self.
explosionCurrentFrame]
                self.image.set_colorkey(self.explosionCkey)
                self.explosionCurrentFrame += 1
            else:
                self.image = pygame.Surface((0, 0))
                self.image.set_colorkey(self.ckey)

            self.respawnTimer -= 1
            if self.respawnTimer <= 0:
                self.reset()
        else:
            # Process player input
            controls = self.getPlayerInput()
```

```
                self.processControl(controls)
                self.image = pygame.transform.rotate(self.asset,
    self.angle)

            # Collision Detection
            self.checkForCollisions()

            # Update Physics
            self.updatePhysics()

    def checkForCollisions(self):
     for gameObject in self.collisionGroup:
            self.collision = self.rect.colliderect(gameObject.rect)
            if self.collision:
                    self.onDeath()
                    for gameObject in self.collisionGroup:
                        gameObject.onDeath()
                    self.waveManager.playerDie()
                    break

    def updatePhysics(self):
     self.velocityX += self.accelerationX
     self.velocityY += self.accelerationY

     # Apply damping horizontal
     if self.velocityX < 0 - self.damping:
            self.velocityX += self.damping
     elif self.velocityX > 0 + self.damping:
            self.velocityX -= self.damping
     else:
            self.velocityX = 0
     # Apply damping vertical
     if self.velocityY < 0 - self.damping:
            self.velocityY += self.damping
     elif self.velocityY > 0 + self.damping:
            self.velocityY -= self.damping
     else:
            self.velocityY = 0

     # Cap maximum velocity
     if self.velocityX > self.maxVelocity:
            self.velocityX = self.maxVelocity
     if self.velocityX < self.maxVelocity * -1:
            self.velocityX - self.maxVelocity * -1
     if self.velocityY > self.maxVelocity:
            self.velocityY =self.maxVelocity
     if self.velocityY < self.maxVelocity * -1:
```

```
            self.velocityY = self.maxVelocity * -1

        self.rect.x += self.velocityX
        self.rect.y += self.velocityY

    def getPlayerInput(self):
        up = pygame.key.get_pressed()[pygame.K_UP]
        right = pygame.key.get_pressed()[pygame.K_RIGHT]
        down = pygame.key.get_pressed()[pygame.K_DOWN]
        left = pygame.key.get_pressed()[pygame.K_LEFT]
        return up, right, down, left

    def processControl(self, control):
        if control[0] and control[3]:
            self.angle = 45
        elif control[0] and control[1]:
            self.angle = 315
        elif control[1] and control[2]:
            self.angle = 225
        elif control[2] and control[3]:
            self.angle = 135
        elif control[0]:
            self.angle = 0
        elif control[1]:
            self.angle = 270
        elif control[2]:
            self.angle = 180
        elif control[3]:
            self.angle = 90
        self.accelerationX = self.thrust * (control[1] - control[3])
        self.accelerationY = self.thrust * (control[2] - control[0])

class Enemy(pygame.sprite.Sprite):
    def __init__(self, image, scale, clip, ckey, screenXY,
    gameObjectTarget, waveManager):
        self.image = imageLoader(image, scale, clip)
        self.image.set_colorkey(ckey)
        self.rect = self.image.get_rect()
        self.rect.x = 200
        self.rect.y = 500
self.accelerationX = 0
        self.accelerationY = 0
        self.velocityX = 0
        self.velocityY = 0
        self.thrust = 0.5
        self.damping = 0.3
        self.maxVelocity = 6
```

```
self.screenX = screenXY[0]
self.screenY = screenXY[1]
self.target = gameObjectTarget
self.isWaitingToRespawn = False
self.respawnTimer = 0
self.detectionRange = 300
self.waveManager = waveManager
self.waveManager.enemyList.append(self)
self.isActive = False
self.onSpawn()

def update(self):
# Check if object is waiting to respawn
if self.isWaitingToRespawn:
        self.respawnTimer -= 1
        if self.respawnTimer <= 0:
            self.reset()
elif not self.isActive:
        self.velocityX = 0
        self.velocityY = 0
else:
        # Check states
        self.processStates()

        # Start Physics
        self.velocityX += self.accelerationX
        self.velocityY += self.accelerationY

# Apply damping horizontal
if self.velocityX < 0 - self.damping:
        self.velocityX += self.damping
elif self.velocityX > 0 + self.damping:
        self.velocityX -= self.damping
        else:
                self.velocityX = 0
# Apply damping vertical
if self.velocityY < 0 - self.damping:
        self.velocityY += self.damping
elif self.velocityY > 0 + self.damping:
        self.velocityY -= self.damping
else:
        self.velocityY = 0

# Cap maximum velocity
if self.velocityX > self.maxVelocity:
        self.velocityX = self.maxVelocity
if self.velocityX < self.maxVelocity * -1:
```

```
            self.velocityX - self.maxVelocity * -1
    if self.velocityY > self.maxVelocity:
            self.velocityY =self.maxVelocity
    if self.velocityY < self.maxVelocity * -1:
            self.velocityY = self.maxVelocity * -1

    # Change position
    self.rect.x += self.velocityX
    self.rect.y += self.velocityY

    # Check bounds
    self.checkBounds()

def checkBounds(self):
    if self.state != 2 and self.isActive and (self.rect.x >= self.
rect.width + self.screenX or self.rect.y >= self.rect.height + self.
screenY):
        self.isActive = False
        self.waveManager.score += 1
        self.onDeath()

def processStates(self):
    # Get target vectors
    targetVectorX = self.target.rect.x - self.rect.x
    targetVectorY = self.target.rect.y - self.rect.y
    distance = math.sqrt((targetVectorX)**2 + (targetVectorY)**2)

    # State one, enemy is searching for player
    if self.state == 1:
     if distance <= self.detectionRange:
            self.state = 2
     else:
            self.accelerationX = self.thrust
            self.accelerationY = self.thrust

    # Enemy is chasing player
    elif self.state == 2:
     if distance > self.detectionRange:
            self.state = 3
     else:
            targetVectorX /= distance
            targetVectorY /= distance
            self.accelerationX = targetVectorX * self.thrust
            self.accelerationY = targetVectorY * self.thrust

    # Enemy lost chase
    elif self.state == 3:
```

```
        self.accelerationX = self.thrust
        self.accelerationY = self.thrust

    def onSpawn(self):
        self.reset()

    def onDeath(self):
        self.waveManager.enemyDie()
        self.isWaitingToRespawn = True
        self.respawnTimer = playerRespawnTimer

    def reset(self):
        self.rect.x = random.randrange(0, self.screenX) * -1
        self.rect.y = random.randrange(0, self.screenY) * -1
        self.velocityX = 0
        self.velocityY = 0
        self.state = 1
        self.isWaitingToRespawn = False

class Asteroid(pygame.sprite.Sprite):
    def __init__ (self, image, scale, clip, ckey, screenXY):
        self.image = imageLoader(image, scale, clip)
        self.image.set_colorkey(ckey)
        self.rect = self.image.get_rect()
        randomVel = random.randrange(2, 5)
        self.velocityX = randomVel
        self.velocityY = randomVel
        self.accelerationX = 0
        self.accelerationY = 0
        self.screenX = screenXY[0]
        self.screenY = screenXY[1]
        self.isWaitingToRespawn = False
        self.respawnTimer = 0
        self.onSpawn()

    def update(self):
        # Check if object is waiting to respawn
        if self.isWaitingToRespawn:
            self.respawnTimer -= 1
            if self.respawnTimer <= 0:
                self.reset()
        else:
            self.velocityX += self.accelerationX
            self.velocityY += self.accelerationY
            self.rect.x += self.velocityX
            self.rect.y += self.velocityY
            if self.rect.x >= self.rect.width + self.screenX or
```

```
                self.rect.y >= self.rect.height + self.screenY:
                            self.reset()


        def onSpawn(self):
            self.reset()


        def onDeath(self):
            self.isWaitingToRespawn = True
            self.respawnTimer = playerRespawnTimer


        def reset(self):
            self.rect.x = random.randrange(0, self.screenX) * -1
            self.rect.y = random.randrange(0, self.screenY) * -1
            self.isWaitingToRespawn = False


    class WaveManager():
        def __init__(self, initWaveSize, maxWaveSize, nextWaveSound):
            self.currentWave = 0
            self.activeNumber = 0
            self.maxWaveSize = maxWaveSize
            self.initWaveSize = initWaveSize
            self.waveSize = self.initWaveSize
            self.enemyList = []
            self.score = 0
            self.nextWaveSound = nextWaveSound


        def activateEnemies(self):
            for enemy in self.enemyList:
                if self.activeNumber < self.waveSize and not enemy.isAc-
    tive:
                    enemy.isActive = True
                    self.activeNumber += 1
        def enemyDie(self):
            self.activeNumber -= 1


        def nextWave(self):
            self.activateEnemies()
            self.currentWave += 1
            if self.currentWave > 1:
                self.nextWaveSound.play()
            if self.waveSize < self.maxWaveSize:
                self.waveSize += 1


        def playerDie(self):
            self.waveSize = self.initWaveSize
            self.currentWave = 0
            self.activeNumber = 0
```

```
        for enemy in self.enemyList:
            enemy.isActive = False

    def update(self):
    if self.activeNumber <= 0:
            self.nextWave()
```

Glossary

Animation	Creating the appearance of movement by making incremental changes to successive images and displaying them in sequence.
Artificial intelligence	In video games, the intelligent behavior of non-playable characters.
Collision detection	Collision detection is determining if an object in your game is in contact with another object.
Event Queue	The event queue is a list of player inputs stored as event objects that we can access with the **pygame.event.get()** function.
Frames Per Second	Frames per second, or FPS, refers to the number of times a display updates every second.
Game Event Logic	Game logic that is associated with a specific event and that executes only when that event occurs.
Game Loop	The pattern of receiving player input, updating the game, and then rendering the game objects that the player is interacting with.
Game Object Logic	Game logic that is associated with a game object and that executes whenever the object is updated in the game loop.
Game Physics	The simulation of motion and interaction specifically designed to address the requirements of a particular game.
Game Progression	The player's advancement through the game, reflected by increasing difficulty, plot progression, increased score, or any of a number of other techniques.
Player Input	The methods used by a game player to interact with the game. Input can include, but is not limted to, keypresses, mouse movements, and gamepads.

Glossary

RGB Value	RGB stands for Red Green Blue, and is a standard way of defining color. Each value can be a number between 0 and 255, with 0 representing no color and 255 representing full color. For example, the RGB for black is 0,0,0 and white is 255,255,255.
Score	A simple method for tracking player progression using a consistently incremented numerical value.
Sound Effects	Audio that is played in response to certain game events, often used to increase player immersion, reinforce game progression, or reward player actions.
Sprites	Sprites are two-dimensional images that are a part of a larger scene and that can be manipulated without modifying the overall scene.
State Machine	An abstract machine that can be in one of a set number of states and can transition to different states according to triggering events or conditions.
Surface	A **surface** is an object that is used to represent any image. Surfaces have a fixed resolution and pixel format.
Thrust	A reaction force that accelerates a system in the opposite direction of mass that has been expelled from that system.
Vector	A mathematical way to describe the movement from one point in space to another.

Join The Development Club

https://learntoprogram.tv/course/ultimate-monthly-bundle/?coupon=BOOK19

$19 ENROLLMENT

This comprehensive membership includes:

☑ Access to EVERY course in LearnToProgram's growing library--including our exciting lineup of new courses planned for the coming year. This alone is over a $3,000 value.

☑ Access to our Live Courses. Take any of our online instructor-led courses which normally cost up to $300. These courses will help you advance your professional skills and learn important techniques in web, mobile, and game development.

☑ Free certification exams. As you complete your courses, earn LearnToProgram's certifications by passing optional exams. All certification fees are waived for club members.

☑ Weekly instructor hangouts where you can ask questions about course material, your personal learning goals, or just chat!

☑ Free Personal Learning Plans. You'll never wonder what you should take next to achieve your goals!

☑ The LearnToProgram guarantee!

Use the coupon code

BOOK19

and save $20 off your first month!

Our Guarantee:
If you watch the course videos and complete the lab exercises, **you will learn to program.** Guaranteed. If you don't, we will personally pay your membership fees for the next 90 days.

THE LEARNTOPROGRAM GUARANTEE

The Development Club

More Information at: *https://LearnToProgram.tv*

www.ingramcontent.com/pod-product-compliance
Lightning Source LLC
Chambersburg PA
CBHW080404060326
40689CB00019B/4123